The
Little Book
of Big Lies

The
Little Book
of Big Lies

A JOURNEY INTO
INNER FITNESS

TINA LIFFORD

AMISTAD

An Imprint of HarperCollinsPublishers

THE LITTLE BOOK OF BIG LIES. Copyright © 2019 by Mary Tina Lifford.
All rights reserved. Printed in the United States of America. No part of
this book may be used or reproduced in any manner whatsoever without
written permission except in the case of brief quotations embodied in critical
articles and reviews. For information, address HarperCollins Publishers,
195 Broadway, New York, NY 10007.

HarperCollins books may be purchased for educational, business, or sales
promotional use. For information, please email the Special Markets
Department at SPsales@harpercollins.com.

Originally published as *The Little Book of Big Lies* in the USA in 2013
by WUF Publishing.

FIRST HARPERCOLLINS PAPERBACK EDITION PUBLISHED IN 2020

Designed by Terry McGrath

Library of Congress Cataloging-in-Publication Data is available
upon request.

ISBN 978-0-06-293029-3

20 21 22 23 24 LSC 10 9 8 7 6 5 4 3 2 1

One morning I woke up to the devastating news that my brother was using heroin. This drug turns users into the walking dead. When I think of the choice my brother made for his life, I think about the lies he ingested that led him to this unhealthy choice. Devastating choices are preceded by the devastating lie that somehow we are not good enough. We swallow this lie whole.

The lie, once ingested, becomes part of us. We speak the lie, we think the lie, and we tell ourselves the lie whether we're conscious of it or not.

This book is for Steve, who now rests in peace.

CONTENTS

FOREWORD

PEOPLE ALL OVER OUR PLANET ARE WAKING UP TO THE truth that there is a great destiny loaded and coded within us all. People are becoming aware that their destiny is not in the hands of seeming external forces, their DNA, their environment, or decisions made by younger versions of themselves. More and more individuals are becoming aware that our life experiences are determined by our beliefs and our perceptions that then form themselves as our life experiences. Holding *The Little Book of Big Lies* in your hands right now indicates that you are indeed ready to take total responsibility for your own happiness, health, success, and prosperity. In fact, you are indeed ready to consciously participate in your own unfolding while relinquishing excuses and incessant complaining about how life has done you wrong.

I have known Tina Lifford for many years. I have watched her put into practice the Universal truths found in her book and observed how her life continues to bear witness to the ever-increasing success and wellbeing in which she genuinely glows. So, *The Little Book of Big Lies* is not just a theoretical treatise that was forced into expression through the intellect. Tina has lived what she is teaching, which makes this book ever more powerful. As you read it you will uncover lies about yourself and about life that you may have unconsciously been living. Remember, a lie believed acts as a law until it's neutralized. Tina will assist you in neutralizing those lies so you can be free to live the life that you are meant to live.

I dare say that everyone has a "meant-to-be" within them. Everyone is filled to overflowing with infinite potential and limitless good. What separates us is our habits, including our mental habits. This book will assist you in changing your mental habits and the lies that helped bring them into being. This seemingly little book is big in what it delivers. It delivers real transformation for those who are willing to not only read it but also practice the inner fitness principles that are clearly laid out for us. It is the Truth that will make us free, and Tina leads us right to it. Now, it's up to you.

Peace and Blessings,
Michael B. Beckwith
Founder, Agape International Spiritual Center
Author, *Spiritual Liberation & Life Visioning*

A Journey into Inner Fitness

Heartfelt sharing helps to unravel lies
and heal and transform our lives.

I AM AN ACTRESS BY PROFESSION. BUT FOR THE PAST THIRTY years, alongside my acting career, my passion for personal development—my own and the field in general—has led me to study how to navigate the mental, emotional, and spiritual challenges human beings face.

My earliest memory of being interested in learning how to live life well dates back to the second grade. I used to walk to school along the edge of the sidewalk so that my friend—God— could walk next to me. I sat at my desk scrunched to one side for the same reason. I loved talking to my friend. I loved talking to people and asking (what I later learned were) uncommon and often uncomfortable questions. Adults often called me an old soul.

I have experienced profoundly touching and healing moments while sitting with myself, with clients, with peers in workshops, and in a master's program in spiritual psychology. I find it both an honor and a gift to listen to people share their hurts, dramas, traumas, upsets, disappointments, and fears. *Hurts, dramas, traumas, upsets, disappointments, and fears* is my phrase for the lies that crash into our lives and make us feel small or fearful. From this perspective any experience or event that leaves us feeling worthless, not good enough, afraid of discovering or being ourselves, or disconnected from our innate value is a lie—a false impression. False impressions are not the truth.

But today, science is discovering ways we can rewire our brains regarding hurts, dramas, traumas, upsets, disappointments, and fears. The reality that we can change the things we have struggled with most of our lives is exciting and important.

The Little Book of Big Lies is a compilation of stories about the inner challenge of being a human being and steps you can take to discover and own your innate power—and start rewiring your response to old challenges and triggers. These stories work together to offer a look at subtle ways you can become disconnected from your sense of innate worth and wind up feeling not good enough. They aim to help you to recognize lies that have made their way into your life and that try to make you feel small or broken. They will give you effective tools for saying "No!" to these lies and "Yes!" to more Self-awareness, Self-acceptance, and Self-care. *Self-care* means acknowledging and honoring your innate worth and tending to the needs of your inner Self.

Each story presents an undeniable, irrefutable truth that can help you reconnect with your Self and take your power back from the challenges you encounter in life. You will learn ways to take new steps to heal old wounds and aim for new possibilities. Each story builds upon the others and is designed to lead you to an awakening of your deeper, innately whole Self.

I have learned that no problem is unique. We are all in this together. Our personal challenges are society's challenges. The details may vary from person to person, but the basic human experience is the same—abuse, feeling unwanted, betrayal, illness, addiction, bad choices, crushing disappointment, unresolved hurt of all kinds.

The good news is that our greatest challenge or pain is also the experience of tens of thousands of others. When we see our personal experiences as reflecting a more common social experience, shame and secrecy become unnecessary and unhelpful.

The realization that we are not alone in our struggles is comforting for most people. The even better news is that countless others have found their way out of the challenges they faced and into more freedom than they ever thought possible. This is the possibility for each of us. The stories in this book celebrate this possibility.

Let's stop turning sadness into shame; let's stop taking the human condition personally. Research tells us that one in four people has experienced some form of parental abuse, one in five Americans was sexually molested as a child, and one in eight grew up with alcoholic relatives. We all have had experiences that dimmed our light, and at times irrational fear has lived in all of us. The best we can do for our Self and society is to learn more about who we are and talk openly (and constructively) about our experiences. When I am not in front of the camera, this is what I do. Through my play *The Circle*, in articles, through writing scripts and facilitating workshops, I look at pain with my eyes focused on resilience and healing.

Talking about our pain and challenges is different from wallowing in them. Wallowing feeds the lie that we're not good enough. Talking about our hurt as part of our commitment to healing will heal and educate us. It will lead us to the personal discovery of *I Am Enough*. We must learn to feel beautiful, capable, and good enough just as we are. This is the residual benefit of inner fitness.

I established The Inner Fitness Project in 2011. It was the third iteration of my desire to create a place where (at that time) women could feel safe, seen, and heard as they tried to find themselves. I called my first effort in this space Totally Fabulous Woman. A few years of working with that name revealed that many women had a difficult time seeing themselves as totally fabulous. For many, the hurt and violations they had experienced made "totally fabulous" an unbelievable leap. When I realized that, the name morphed into Waking Up Fabulous. This felt better because, after all, doesn't everyone want to wake up the fabulousness that lives inside of them? Women loved that name, and I began to design and facilitate workshops to serve those women.

But something was still missing. I couldn't put my finger on it until the morning I awakened and the words *inner fitness* greeted me. They were etched on the inside of my eyelids. I saw them and spoke them and smiled. These words perfectly say what I have been trying to say for years: Our inner fitness is important. Inner fitness is the journey we all yearn for, women and men, without knowing it—to wake up from the relentless harassment of the naysaying, Self-doubting inner critic. I saw that *inner fitness* was a term and an idea that could serve humanity. I became obsessed with learning, comparing, and creating strategies that foster inner fitness.

I grew up watching famed fitness guru Jack LaLanne bring physical wellness strategies into homes across America. He was the first person to open a gym in the United States, back in 1936. He touted the positive impact that physical exercise has on our overall physical health, strength, and wellness. His efforts changed lives for the better. His efforts even educated a doubting medical community.

If placing an emphasis on physical fitness had transformed, in fewer than eighty-five years, how the world approaches physical wellness, what would happen to our wellbeing if we turned our attention inward and took the stand that *inner fitness* is as important as physical fitness? Would the wellbeing of our families and nation increase? *(Note that I prefer to spell* wellbeing *without the hyphen. It makes the word look stronger, unbroken— the way we all want to be stronger and feel whole and unbroken.)*

I hope you find relief in these stories and use them as building blocks for your inner fitness. They come from my personal life, from interviews I have conducted, and from the lives of clients I have coached over the past twenty years. They are meant to help free you from the little lies that compromise inner strength and wellbeing and encourage you to dare to reach for new possibilities for your Self.

The truth in each story will set you free, *if you practice it*— the same way push-ups will make you stronger if you do them. Follow the "Try This" inner fitness exercises at the end of each chapter, and you will transform old patterns into new personal power.

* * *

I hope *The Little Book of Big Lies* will become a place where you feel safe, seen, and heard and that the truths on its pages will SET YOU FREE and fill you with an endless sense of new possibilities.

* * *

There is no greater purpose
than to engage the journey
back to your Self.

Finding Your True Self

Developing our awareness of our inner
Self, the innately whole and worthy part of us,
makes all the other tasks and events in life easier.

THE PERSON INSIDE OF YOU WHO WAKES UP, STRUGGLES with life, feels overwhelmed and at war, and needs to be in control is not who you really are at your core. **This warring outer self is our small surviving self—a distortion.**

Distortions are lies.

They are like the images we see in a House of Mirrors at an amusement park. The mirrors make our images so grotesque, weird, or laughable that we barely recognize ourselves. In one mirror we look like the Pillsbury Doughboy, and in another our heads are pointy and our faces elongated and wavy.

When I was growing up, my family regularly visited an amusement park in Chicago called Riverview Park. The House of Mirrors was a family favorite. There were always a couple of mirrors in which the distortion was so captivating that I found myself fixed in one spot—twisting my body from side to side, distending my belly, and making weird faces to see what the distorted mirror would reflect.

But I also got bored with seeing myself distorted and was usually the first person who wanted to leave the House of Mirrors. Once the novelty of the weird shapes wore off, I was ready to be myself and move on. I wanted to get on with the fun of the day and enjoy the other attractions and rides.

So, normally, after maybe five minutes in the attraction, I was eager to get to the last mirror. It was usually placed by itself, just on the other side of a curtain. This last mirror was not a trick mirror. It told the truth and marked the end of the attraction. When I looked in the last mirror, a certain calm always settled over me as I saw myself again as I really was, undistorted. I would shake my head at the thought of how awful it would be to get stuck inside a House of Mirrors forever and never have a clear image of myself.

* * *

When I was in my twenties, I was obsessed with figuring life out. *(Now I have to stop for a moment. I have learned to stop myself and tell a deeper truth whenever a statement I make calls for it. The deeper truth here is that my obsession with figuring life out was based in fear. I was afraid of all that could go wrong in life. I was afraid of change. I was afraid that life might throw something my way that I could not handle—the death of my parents, a devastating betrayal, becoming a person I didn't know how to be. I wanted to*

*have a jump on life so it would not catch me off guard and drag me
to a place from which I could not return.)*

Instinctively, I knew there was more to my life than the
rush-rush and day-to-day thoughts of career, dating, and making money that were my focus then. I was making strides in
virtually every area of my life, yet my accomplishments fell
short of fulfilling the satisfying "something" that eluded me.
I longed to feel a sense of inner fulfillment that was different
from feeling proud of my worldly accomplishments. I began
fervently searching for this something.

My thirties were a time of awakening. Every book I read
and every lecture or spiritual retreat I attended gave me another piece to the puzzle of life. I realized that life is indeed a
House of Mirrors—full of captivating distortions that lie to us
and keep us from seeing ourselves as perfect and whole just as
we are. I had once heard Michael Bernard Beckwith refer to
human beings as innately perfect, whole, and complete. This
notion felt correct to me, and I began to work inside of myself
to understand and embody it.

In life there is but one overarching task. It is to discover the
truth of who we are. Developing our awareness of our inner
Self, the innately thriving, whole, and worthy part of us, makes
all other tasks and challenges in life events easier.

* * *

In my search for this "something," I began to catch myself
thinking and behaving in ways that were no longer a fit for

the life I wanted. Engaging in gossip, judging and finding fault, distrusting everything and everybody started to make my life feel small. These habits had been so comfortable I didn't realize they were habits. I believed my thoughts and behavior were just "me." It never occurred to me to challenge them until I started to feel their restriction. I also felt confined when people would place *their* limitations on me, discount my thoughts or feelings, and tell me how I should think or be. I was desperate to find a way of being with life that was a fit for *me*.

About this time I was introduced to one of my all-time favorite spiritual quotations (by Ernest Holmes): *Faith is the most important thing in your life. It is impossible to arrive at the grandeur of its possibility through petty thinking and small ideas.*

When I developed the ability to see how often my thinking and behavior were rooted in varying degrees of fear and pettiness, I began to reach for a new and bigger possibility. I became determined to find my way to freedom. I resolved to trade fear for the inner grit life requires.

I did not know exactly what it meant or looked like to forge a relationship with my Self, but the promise of profound inner resilience, Self-acceptance, and peace was the carrot I chased.

* * *

When my mind is working on a problem, it is not uncommon for me to go to bed with a particular question and wake up having dreamed the answer. In my forties, I had a dream that opened the door wide to a new way of seeing my Self (with a capital *S*).

In the dream I was on a secluded beach looking for something. It was an overcast day. Up ahead I saw two women arguing. One was standing facing the endless ocean, and the other's back was to the water. As I got closer to them, I realized that only one woman was arguing. The one facing the water was listening. Actually, the more accurate statement is that the one facing the water was just standing there, exquisitely *being*, while the arguing one was very animated—shouting, stomping, cursing.

To me, the quiet, listening one was the more compelling. I was drawn to her. The closer I got to the two of them, the more animated the arguing one became. It was as if her flailing arms and loud voice were desperately trying to distract me—pull my focus to her and away from the quietly present one. I could see the arguing one's mouth moving, but I did not hear her words, even as I moved closer and closer.

The quiet one's radiance was like a magnet pulling me to her. Willingly, I complied.

I stopped about ten feet away from them. The compelling woman turned toward me and smiled in a knowing way. Then, she stepped toward the arguing one and embraced her. As they held one another, they both turned to look at me. I saw they were both me. In that moment the overcast clouds parted, and the sun broke through, shining so brightly it blinded me for a moment. When I could see again, both women had disappeared.

* * *

I woke from that dream energized. It had revealed that the something I was looking for was my Self.

Yes. I could clearly see my *selves* in this dream. I could see that in my daily life, I was constantly moving in and out of these three selves. I had never thought of myself in terms of the parts that I saw in the dream. Yet, there I was: Three distinct parts of me were on that beach—all living together in the same moment.

Seeing myself in this way felt instructive. I named these three selves the *surviving self*, the *thriving Self*, and the *infinite SELF*. Seeing them, and then paying attention to them in my life, has transformed how I see my Self and others.

* * *

The surviving self is the arguing self in the dream. I knew her flailing arms, loud voice, and tendency to feel upset. The surviving self represents the part of me (the part of all of us) that reacts to life. She is quick to judge and take things personally and is always ready for a fight—attacking, proving, protecting, or blaming.

For this self nothing is ever enough. No matter how well things are going, the surviving self looks for what is wrong. No matter how beautiful the image of Self is in the mirror, this self tends to skip over the good, searching for a problem, or an issue that could potentially become a problem. She sees the image in the mirror as mere flesh and bones and therefore constantly fears for its safety. Thus, the surviving self, regardless of our level of financial abundance or elevated life circumstances, is caught in an endless state of surviving life—doubting, worrying, and resisting. *(In all fairness, I should point out that the reactionary nature of the surviving self is rooted in the reptilian part of our brains. For nearly five hundred million years the role of this part of the brain has been to be on the lookout for danger and to react appropriately.)*

The thriving Self is the image constantly moving forward on the beach of life. Yes! I knew her, too. The thriving Self gives us the ability to hope, dream, and make new choices and to see ourselves as connected to something more powerful than our anxious thoughts. She was the part of me that felt restrained by gossip and my judgmental thinking at that time.

Unlike the surviving self, the thriving Self can observe and create distance between the Self and the events that take place in our lives. This Self can be in difficult circumstances and not feel defined or limited by them. The lives of leaders like Jesus, Mahatma Gandhi, Martin Luther King Jr., and Nelson Mandela confirm this notion of the thriving Self. The thriving Self sees every situation as an opportunity to grow and expand and believes that anything and everything can change for the better. This Self navigates life using as its powerful tools compassion, compassionate action, curiosity, a sense of possibility, enthusiasm, expectation, hope, openness, optimism, vulnerability, acceptance, unity, community, the ability to observe ourselves in action, and the willingness to change.

The profoundly peaceful infinite SELF took my breath away as I witnessed her effortless ability to just *be*. The infinite SELF is the quietly present compelling Self that stands before life unaffected by the chaos of human confusion and fear. I can't help but see this Self as God. This infinite SELF is the essence of life that has existed since the beginning of time. Like clay, SELF morphs into endless forms without its essence ever changing. It is at the center of all things and every human being, and because of it, everything in life is connected. It is the intelligent force behind everything. The infinite SELF is the essence of life that dwells in all of us and everything.

When I learned that the brain's number one function is to support our survival, I saw that the surviving self survives through fear and the thriving Self survives through hope, courage, and curiosity. These are two distinctly different ways of navigating life that leave us with two distinctly different internal experiences. The infinite SELF, on the other hand, being *infinite* and *eternal*, transcends the notion of survival. There is nothing for the infinite SELF to survive because it is life itself. The infinite SELF in us is not at war with life because it *is* life.

It became my goal to make more room for the peace of the infinite SELF, to recognize when I am operating from fear and instead aim to see every situation in life as an opportunity to grow and expand into more of who I am (and to have fun in the process—even in those moments when life might drop me to my knees). This notion taught me to constantly ask myself the question, *Are you looking at life from a place of fear, curiosity, or acceptance—from the surviving self, the thriving Self, or the infinite SELF?*

Today, when I observe my surviving self taking the reins, I know to consciously shift my energy and thinking toward thriving characteristics: become curious about my circumstances; ask my Self how I can use the situation before me to grow and expand; ask what might be possible beyond what I see; accept that whatever life brings to my plate is mine to handle and grow from; trust that my inner Self, steeped in the infinite nature of God, can guide me. This is the starting point for strengthening our relationship with Self. This is the inner fitness practice I defer to.

* * *

In the dream, when the compelling woman embraced the flailing argumentative self, her act revealed a purpose encoded in us all:

> Acknowledge the inner Self. Embrace the idea that we have innate value, and our innate strength, wisdom, and love will throw its arms around the unhappy surviving self, and our experience of life will transform.

The goal of knowing my Self jumped ahead of all other goals. Having a career, a house, and great relationships remained important, but not as important or fulfilling as the discovery of this inner oasis and power.

* * *

I have fallen in love with the ability of the thriving Self to rethink, rechoose, and rewrite the past. Contemplating the infinite SELF teaches me that I am innately capable of meeting any circumstance and that nothing in life can destroy the infinite part of me.

My dream of Self does not mean that old habits stop presenting themselves. But seated in a higher sense of Self, I see even the most nuanced Self-rejection and abusive tendencies quickly, and I head them off at the pass. It has become much easier for me to interrupt the habits of the surviving self and to work to retrain and rewire my reactions. When a negative thought tries to land and take root in my life, I know it is a lie, and I make no room for it. If a lie happens to take root and grow, I pull it out as soon as I see it.

I don't pretend that problems and fears don't exist. I simply, as the Dalai Lama says, pay them no mind—I give them no meaning. I invest no energy that would create for them a greater reality.

Self with a capital *S* is teaching me that I can change my relationship to anything. This makes me more courageous and determined. If I encounter difficult people or situations, a relationship breakup or other challenging events that disturb my sense of myself, I question my surviving self perspective and work to shift it.

The aim is not to get rid of the surviving self. This self is quite helpful. Over the course of human history it has taught us to sense and survive all kinds of threats. Also, this is the self that can get deliciously caught up in the moment and common notions of romantic love. The aim is to have a relationship with my Self that allows me to better manage the surviving self.

Up until now the surviving self has gotten way too much of our attention. The goal is to pay more attention to the thriving Self and the infinite SELF.

Like the mirrors I stood before in the House of Mirrors, I have come to assign the label of "trick mirror" to anything that tries to distort my healthy vision of myself. This reminds me to see all pain as a distortion, and not the truth. **I look for the lies that have snagged me and turn to my Self in navigating them.**

I have cultivated a circle of girlfriends where I feel safe, seen, and heard—just like the characters in my play *The Circle*. *The Circle* is about seven diverse women learning to navigate the choppy waters of life together. For five years I contemplated writing it. (*Actually, the deeper truth is that for five years I doubted my ability to write the characters and stories that were rustling around inside of me begging for life. I didn't consider myself a writer. My mind kept looking for someone else—a "real" writer—to step in and bring the characters to life. Finally, I realized one of life's biggest lessons: No one can step in and do for us what is ours to do—whether it is writing a play or rewriting our personal stories of hurt. Being afraid does not let us off the hook. This realization was a point of demarcation on the journey to my Self: If no one can step in and do my work for me, and life is short, and I want to be fully alive, then*

I must throw my arms around my surviving self, dive into my life with hope in my heart, and nurture new possibilities in my mind. Courageously stretching beyond my comfort zone to apply this new way of being in my life opened a door through which both this book and The Circle *were born. Since the reading of the first draft of* The Circle *by a group of actresses in 2011, the play has been performed in eight cities for thousands of people. It has been changing people's lives, proving to me that learning to lovingly manage the surviving self is the shortest distance between where we are and where we want to be.)*

My real-life circle and I have made a pact to support one another. We act as an undistorted mirror for each other. When the habits of the surviving self grab hold, we help one another to see how the surviving self is in control so that we can then make thriving-Self choices. We look to one another to remember that we are beautiful, whole, and undistorted.

My real-life circle has so enriched my life that I wanted to turn our experience into a theatrical one that audiences everywhere could enjoy and benefit from. It is gratifying to witness audience members see themselves in the characters in *The Circle* and boldly throw their voices into the room when, toward the end of the play, they get to shout to every dream stealer who has ever hurt them, "Carry your own damn bag!"

The two statements that above all others have helped me come to know that each of us is more than the image we see in the mirror are (1) God don't make junk, and (2) there is a part of us that can never be hurt, harmed, or endangered.

This part is the infinite SELF, the force I call God. The idea that this force lives inside of me as the infinite SELF is more than comforting. It gives me permission to challenge any and every fear and to trust that life works with itself for the benefit of itself.

As I hiked up a mountain one overcast morning, my dream replayed in my mind. I got to the part when the compelling woman embraces the arguing one, and the clouds parted, and the sun broke through. But this day when the dream was replaying, for the first time, when the sun broke through the clouds and the light was so bright that the two women disappeared, I realized that they did not disappear. Instead, we all became one. This is the possibility for each of us—that the three selves work together harmoniously as one.

Our true purpose is to discover our oneness with the highest SELF—God—the omniscient, intelligent force that governs the universe.

Inner Fitness Practice

The Big Lie

The self you see in the mirror is all that you are.

The Truth

You are so much more than the image you see in
the mirror. The all-pervading intelligent nature and
power that governs the universe lives inside of you.
Give it room, and its presence will expand.

The Possibility

Becoming aware of the Self in you that is full of
possibility, born to thrive, and cannot be hurt,
harmed, or endangered.

Try This

Find a comfortable place in your home to experiment
with feeling the presence of your inner Self:

1. Sit in a chair and become aware of yourself.
   Scan yourself. Become aware of your body. Look
   at your arms. Watch your chest rise and fall. See
   your thighs. Become aware of your calves, legs,
   and feet.

2. Now close your eyes and let go of the image of your body and give no thought to breathing. Become aware of the essence of *you*. Feel it radiating with aliveness. With your eyes closed, see yourself looking at your body without being your body.

3. Say to yourself, *There is more to me than I know.*

*Your inner Self is real
and can stand up to anything
that happens in life.*

The Truth About Lies

When we let in anyone's dark lies, and
choose to believe them, we distort our
natural God-given wholeness.

Dictionary.com: Lie

noun

1. A false statement made with deliberate intent to deceive; an intentional untruth; a falsehood.
2. Something intended or serving to convey a false impression; imposture.
3. An inaccurate or false statement.

verb (used without an object)

4. To speak falsely or utter untruth knowingly, as with intent to deceive.
5. To express what is false; to convey a false impression.

NOT ALL LIES ARE EQUAL. SOME ARE FUN. I LOVE CALLING a good friend or family member and spinning a tale like,

"We're on our way to Vegas to get married!" I enjoy saying, "Gotcha!" when they believe me.

Some lies are white lies—little "fibs" that don't harm any-one—like telling a friend on the phone, when we don't want to talk to that person at the time, "Oh, someone's at the door; I'll call you back later." Then we hang up the phone and continue watching television or doing whatever we were doing before their call.

Then there are the other lies—the ones that are mean and damaging. Lies like, "You're not worth the time of day." That was the lie repeatedly told to my coaching client Carol by her mother. Saundra, another client, was told by her church that being gay was a terrible disease only curable by obedient faith. My client Kathy's lie—"You're stupid"—was handed to her by her siblings when she flunked the third grade and they brutally teased her.

Then there's my client Brenda, who spent her twenties en-gaged in promiscuous behavior because her uncle molested her when her parents were not around one night. He lied to her about her Self-worth, telling her that nasty things happen to nasty girls.

All kinds of lies clutter our lives. I call these *dark lies*. They attach themselves to our minds and hearts and, like vam-pires, suck our precious strength—leaving us empty, insecure, filled with fear, limited in some other way, or feeling not good enough. These dark lies enter our lives from the mouths of par-ents and caregivers, teachers, friends, and society generally. But they stay in our lives because we begin to tell ourselves—and believe—some version of those lies.

After twenty years of peering deep into my own beliefs and working with the deeply rooted beliefs of my coaching clients, **I am convinced that underneath every chronic frustration or emotional pain lives a lie we were told that we now tell to ourselves.**

Writing this book—my first one—was a frustrating, confounding experience until I saw the lie living underneath my procrastination and writer's block: I was afraid that readers would find me "too much . . . too serious"—words my older teenage cousins used to reject me. Boys I was interested in did the same. Even my father found it hard to be alone with me when I was a little girl because I was prone to ask deep, difficult questions that made him have to stop, think, and talk about things that he found uncomfortable.

For years, the lie of "you're too much" sat on my desire to write. It caused me to doubt or second-guess the value of what I passionately wanted to say. Whenever I was in a conversation and sensed uninterest surfacing, inwardly I would tell myself, *You're being too much . . . too serious.*

* * *

If we look closely at what scares us, or what makes us feel overwhelmed to the point that we sometimes just want to give up, we'll find a lie that we are repeatedly telling ourselves. These lies that hold us down and distort what's possible for our lives are easy to see once we know what to look for—the message or belief that tells us we're not good enough.

The way I see it, any statement that negatively impacts our Self-esteem is a lie—an inaccurate way of seeing our Self. Let me explain: Start with the first statement I mentioned above: "God don't make junk." That truth means that any point of view, ours or someone else's, that says we are unworthy, incapable, inconsequential, or talentless is false; it's a lie to be unceremoniously uprooted from our lives and replaced with the truth: "God don't make junk."

Lies, by definition, are inaccuracies, simply false statements—until we take them into our hearts and begin to treat ourselves as though the lies we've been told are true.

* * *

Going back to the clients I mentioned above: When Carol's mother told her "You're not worth the time of day," this lie was merely the rant of an unhappy, alcoholic parent. Those angry words had little to do with Carol—until Carol took those words to heart. She began to treat herself the way her mother had treated her. Whenever Carol was frustrated or challenged by trying to achieve something, she would tell herself, "You're not worth the time of day."

Similarly, the dark lie my client Saundra was told, about her homosexuality being a disease, was an uneducated, grossly inaccurate statement. Unfortunately, Saundra let those words into her heart and began to feel shame about her sexuality, and then rejected herself in the same way her priest had rejected her. Little did she know that years later her judgmental, lying priest would be entangled in accusations regarding his own sexuality. Often, we tend to hate in others what we have not or cannot accept about ourselves.

Kathy, after flunking the third grade and being laughed at by her siblings, became a perfectionist who called herself stupid any time she could not do something perfectly or grasp a skill quickly.

Brenda slept with man after man, abusing herself the way her uncle had abused her. She treated herself as though the lie he told her about how nasty things happen to nasty girls like her was true.

By now, I think you get my point: A lie by any other name, even when told by people we love, or by people who are supposed to love us, is still a lie. *These lies can't damage us until we let them into our hearts as truths.*

We must learn to clearly see the lies that are thrown at us. We must call them by their proper name: false or inaccurate statements—*lies*—and reject them so they don't become our truth.

The starting point for transforming the lies that crash into our lives is to become aware of them. Take a moment to observe yourself throughout your day and begin to notice the false and unloving statements, conclusions, and assumptions you have bought into. Become aware of subtle ways you abuse, neglect, or reject your innate worth. This behavior constitutes a rejection of your Self—the sacred, whole, and worthy part of you.

Seeing this previously unconscious behavior toward Self makes you ready to change your mind. The next step in building your inner fitness is to stop in the middle of the old ways of thinking, acknowledge your old unwanted reactions, and then consciously choose more empowering thoughts, more Self-love, more Self-acceptance, and new possibilities. When you feel yourself beginning to engage in a pattern of Self-sabotage or doubt, or an old fear is replaying in your mind or body, interrupt that behavior. Literally, stop and say out loud to yourself: *This is an old pattern. It is a lie that I no longer have to engage.* Calling the behavior out—naming it—makes space for your rational Self to wrestle the reactionary flailing self to the ground. When you can see your dance with the boogeyman, he's not as scary. Instead, tell yourself: *I am capable of moving beyond this habit. I can breathe through my discomfort.*

Imagining what you want or the person you want to become allows your mind to pivot and rise into a higher sense of Self and brain function. You can teach yourself to say *I see you* to every lie that haunts you and pass through old discomfort into a more accurate and nurturing Self-perception.

* * *

A number of years ago I had an experience that taught me I could decide to walk away from the lies that enter my life.

I was coming out of a store on Pico Boulevard in Los Angeles when a homeless man asked me for money. I fished through my pocket for the dollar bill I knew was there. I was happy to hand it to him, imagining that somewhere, someone might be extending a similar kindness to my brother, Steve.

Before Steve's eventual death from a drug overdose, our family experienced long stretches of time when we did not know whether he was dead or alive. He had struggled with drugs off and on since he was fourteen years old. I am certain his real struggle was with the lies he lived with regarding his Self-worth. Steve could not read. The shame and sense of inadequacy this caused left him feeling not good enough in this fiercely competitive world.

But the homeless man who approached me was nothing like my kind and bighearted brother. This homeless man felt entitled to more. He looked at me and surmised that I could do better than a dollar, and told me so. "Ah girl, I see how you're dressed. You can do better than a dollar." I was stunned by his remark. Something was not right about this picture. Generosity is supposed to be followed by a smile or a thank-you. It took a minute for his words to sink in and make sense.

For a brief period—one–one thousand, two–one thousand— I felt like I was in the *Twilight Zone*, where suddenly life takes a bizarre twist. I mentally organized the facts floating in my mind:

1. This man was homeless.

2. I was giving him money—sure, not enough to transform his life, but it was a kind gesture.

3. The appropriate response is "Thank you," not "You can do better."

4. The only thing I owe this man is respect.

When I pulled myself out of the *Twilight Zone*, I told the demanding man in front of me, "I don't owe you anything!" But he kept demanding more. Well, that made no sense to me at all; nor did I have time to stand there arguing the point. I snatched my dollar back and told him I would not pay him to abuse me. He kept yelling at me, calling me names and saying I was selfish, but I did not take into my heart any of the lies—the false statements—he tried to hand me. Instead, I gave him a view of my back . . . as I walked away. *(This was my version of the "talk to the hand" gesture that says don't talk to me because I'm not listening to what you have to say.)* He continued throwing disparaging comments (lies) my way. But his false statements hit my back and fell to the ground at his own feet as I went on with my day.

I can imagine you thinking: *It's easy to ignore a homeless man's ranting. His words don't mean anything. He can't affect how I feel about myself.* Well, I disagree. Harsh words spoken by anyone, no matter how sane or insane, have the power to hurt us if we let them hit that place inside of us that is already tender with Self-doubt. When we let in anyone's dark lies and choose to believe them, we distort our natural God-given wholeness and wind up in pain.

The difference between how we respond to that homeless

man and how we respond, for instance, to a parent saying "You are not worth the time of day" is that we don't let the homeless man's words in. We turn our backs on him and walk away.

But where parents, loved ones, and early childhood experiences are concerned, we haven't realized we must treat their hurtful words and behavior—lies—in the same way. We must learn to see our Self as innately whole and worthy and choose how we allow our Self to be treated by others. Mostly, we must realize that every time we tell our Self the dark lies that were told to us, it is equivalent to the Twilight Zone of paying that homeless man to abuse me.

Use my experience as a metaphor. We must honor and protect our sense of Self by walking away from the crazy rants and lies of others . . . no matter who they are. We must learn to work with our areas of hurt and discomfort in order to reclaim ourselves from the lies we were told . . . we must stop repeating those lies to ourselves . . . we must walk away and get on with our lives.

Inner Fitness Practice

The Big Lie

The mean and damaging things you tell yourself, or that others have told you, are true.

The Truth

Words cannot hurt you. It is the hurtful things you believe about your Self, no matter where they originated, that cause you pain.

The Possibility

Seeing your Self clearly. Loving what you see. Letting go of any lie that has ever hurt you.

Try This

1. When you encounter pain at the end of someone's words, as soon as possible, take a private moment and have a loving conversation with your Self. See their words and actions as a distorted mirror that lies.

2. Tell yourself the TRUTH: God don't make junk. You are innately worthy. Take the opportunity to give yourself a hug.

3. Ask this question out loud to God, or the universe (which is always listening): *How can I thrive in spite of the hurt or discomfort I feel or have experienced?*

Your task is to see the lies and remember that you are more.

11 Questions for Unpacking the Lies That Make You Feel Sad or Small

Lies, lies, and more lies—
where do they all come from?

Are You Thinking That Some Pain Lasts Forever?

No matter how difficult the past,
you can always begin again today.

—JACK KORNFIELD, *BUDDHA'S LITTLE*
INSTRUCTION BOOK

THERE IS ONE STATE THAT EVERY PERSON ON THE PLANET has visited at least once. What state am I talking about? The state of "forever." It's that state of mind where we fear that we will have to live with some kind of pain *forever*. Failed attempts at change, freedom, or forgiveness lead us to this conclusion.

For years, my pain regarding my brother was this kind of "forever" pain. It was a relentless burden. But in the end it taught me some of my most cherished lessons and exposed a big lie—some pain lasts forever—that I had to stop telling my-self.

Almost any way you look at it, "forever" is a lie. It is a truly gross lie when it is the state we live in regarding a past hurt, drama, trauma, upset, disappointment, or fear. When it comes to a chronic area of challenge, thinking about it as a "forever" state, like it will forever be an issue in our lives, is debilitating.

My brother, Steve, was two years older than me. He was the only boy in a family with three smart, go get 'em girls. When we were kids, Steve teased me, pulled my hair, and called me names. But as we grew to become adults, there was never a question about his love for me and mine for him.

The questions I did have were questions for God. And my list was long: Why did Steve, the only boy, get saddled with so many burdens? Why did life have to be so unfair? How can I save my brother? How can I help him feel his worth and value? Why is my life so good and Steve's so challenged? How can I be free of the pain I feel regarding my brother? How can I make peace with it all?

* * *

My brother was what society calls a drug addict. He started smoking marijuana when he was eleven or twelve years old. At fourteen he was "dropping" pills. In his twenties he started shooting heroin, and he did that for ten years. Then crack co-caine was his drug of choice until it killed him. He died face-down on the back seat of his car from a drug overdose fewer than two weeks out of rehab.

I don't like the term *drug addict* because society tends to think that drug addicts are irresponsible—like they haphazardly throw their lives away because they are lazy and cannot just stop using drugs. This is an easy perspective to take. I know. I saw through this lens at one point. But knowledge, time, and compassion have taught me that this perspective did not apply to my brother—nor, no doubt, to countless others.

I know I will sound like a protective sister, but Steve had a lot of "bad hands" dealt to him: For instance, he could not read. Why? I don't know. I can tell you that my father also could not read. This was a secret Daddy managed to keep from the world his whole life. He kept it from my mother for the first eight years of their marriage. I was probably ten or eleven when I realized my father could not read. Smart, streetwise people can hide this disability, unless someone knows what to look for.

I put the pieces together after years of noticing that my mother wrote all the checks and read all mail notices to Daddy. My father was very smart. Not book smart, but smart-smart. He could figure things out. He was wildly creative and had a wisdom that is the fountain from which springs my own old soul. But Daddy's ego and shame made him the wrong person to father a son like my brother.

Steve did not navigate his disability as handily as Daddy seemingly did. It got in his way at school. When a teacher and my mother tried to address this, and a family therapy session was recommended, Daddy went . . . once. But then he forbade Mommy or Steve to ever go again. My mother lived years carrying the pain of regret for having capitulated to that decision and to my father's will.

As for my father, I feel certain that he never talked to his only son about the disability they shared. As much as Daddy had learned to work around it, his inability to read caused him shame. And as is often the case in scenarios like this, his own unaddressed pain made seeing himself in his son hard to bear. This made Daddy hard on Steve . . . even mean to him. *(This is one of those times when I must stop and state a deeper truth: I used to refer, like here, to my father's behavior toward Steve as "mean"; however, the more accurate words might be "wrong" and "abusive." Certainly "insensitive." But as I grew older, I could see and feel how much my father loved my brother. I could also see how completely inadequate my father felt in dealing with Steve's needs. His only answer was to try to toughen Steve up.)*

Daddy's hardness with Steve sometimes included his fist. This was discipline my father never leveled on us girls. A fist is not a method of discipline any human being should have to endure no matter how many cars they steal, days they ditch school, lies they tell . . . or pills they start dropping at a tender age.

Add to my brother's plate the reality that his three sisters were great readers. In fact, we were great at everything. Being great at stuff and being looked up to is supposed to be the big brother's role. When life ends up being different from what we expect, or secrets develop because the truth is not acknowledged or talked about, we develop dis-ease. How do we learn to reconcile that dis-ease? What happens to that unaddressed hurt? How do we learn to cope?

For these and many other reasons, it is hard for me to simply shrug my shoulders and label Steve a drug addict who made lazy choices. But the point of Steve's addiction here is to highlight the burdensome pain I carried because of it. I hurt for so long behind my brother's life that I actually started to believe that the pain I felt would be with me forever.

It's hard not to see something as forever when that thing has been a point of anxiety *forever.*

The life my brother lived was taking a toll on my heart. I was quick to jump when the phone rang late at night. I was ready to fight when someone judged him.

Every year I tried a new approach to setting myself free from the pain I carried for Steve. One year I told myself I just would not care. Another year I swore to never again give him money. Once, I convinced myself that his struggles were just like those that everyone has to overcome.

Year after year, for more than twenty years, my mind and heart would strike out on some strategy meant to free me of the pain related to my brother. Nothing worked. I would almost say that not even prayer worked. But it was prayer that led me to two phrases that changed things and shored up my inner fitness: *up until now* and *from this point forward.* These two phrases proved to me that "forever" is a lie. They paved the way to a freedom that I had yearned for most of my life.

"Forever" sends the message that nothing can be done, that no matter what you try, forever doesn't change. You're stuck with whatever the issue is—weight, Self-esteem, depression, childhood trauma, family dynamics, guilt . . . you name it. "Forever" says, snidely and insensitively, *This is just the way things are.* Worse, *This is who you are.*

But *up until now* and *from this point forward* say, *Just hold your horses, Forever! This may be the way it's been UP UNTIL NOW, but FROM THIS POINT FORWARD, things can change. Something beyond this is possible. And don't you forget it!*

* * *

I first heard the perspective of *up until now* and *from this point forward* in a Spiritual Psychology master's degree program offered at the University of Santa Monica. Here's how it works: *Up until now*, life has been however it's been; but *from this point forward*, everything can change—for the better.

That's it—simple and elegant.

The beauty in *up until now* and *from this point forward* is that this kind of thinking makes room for possibility, opens a door where hope has been lost. It conditions our thinking, and our thinking affects everything else.

Opening the door to a new possibility is a first step. *Up until now* and *from this point forward* do not require that we know what to do once the door is open. When we are open to a new possibility, our willingness carries its own magic. This is what is meant by the saying, "Our job is the *what*; God's job is the *how*." The "how" will manifest once room is made for the possibility.

When added to the front end of our old conversation(s), *up until now* creates new possibilities because it stops us in our tracks and challenges our old "forever" thinking, and that challenge is continued with *from this point forward*. Interrupting our unwanted patterns and making room for new ways of thinking and behaving are foundational to changing our lives.

This is how we can use this pair of phrases to transform our lives: When we are in the midst of talking to ourselves or others and we catch ourselves taking the same old stance, engaging the same old beliefs, seeing in the same old ways, stop. Rethink and restate using *up until now* and *from this point forward*.

I began using this simple tool whenever I spoke about my brother. If I was about to say something like, "Steve's addiction causes me and my family great pain," I'd stop myself and restate the sentence: "*Up until now*, Steve's addiction has caused me and my family great pain." Do you see the glimmer of possibility sitting in this restated sentence? Its light says that change is possible, *from this point forward*. It points to the promise that our challenging experience of things as they have been can, and will, change.

When I restated that thought for the first time, that hint of possibility felt great. Hopeful. And that glimmer grew into new feelings regarding my brother, addiction, and my own life. It wound up taking me to levels of acceptance I had not imagined possible.

Up until now and *from this point forward* are not magical phrases; they are a practical way of shaking free of the "forever" mindset that traps us. Underneath forever's oppressive weight are endless possibilities; therefore, our job is to break ground, and break through.

First, I had to be open to trying *up until now* on for size. But the bigger choice was to make a pact with myself to catch sight of those thoughts that had fallen into a "forever" state. Such thoughts are not easy to see. Unconscious behavior is the hardest to see. **When we are blind to what we do, seeing becomes a precious gift, an event to be celebrated, because we cannot change what we cannot see.**

I made a pact with myself by simply saying to myself, *I am ready to see any thought that is holding me hostage to this pain.* This heartfelt intention watched over my life and helped me to hear my own words and see my own actions so that I could apply *up until now* and *from this point forward* as often as necessary.

Eventually, this vigilance changed my life. It helped me to see how I had taken on a responsibility for my brother that did not belong to me. I saw that I was judging him, holding him to a standard of behavior that worked for *my* life. But Steve and I were different people, and my judgments ignored that fact. We had vastly different experiences although we grew up in the same house. *Who would I be if I had worn his shoes?* I saw that every time I tried to fix Steve or judge his actions, I was implying that he was broken . . . not good enough. A part of me was playing God. That is a role too complex for me to even fathom.

I had to let go of trying to "right" perceived wrongs and let Steve grope his way to his higher power. As I let go and trusted that indeed a higher power cared for Steve just as he was, peace rolled into my life like the dawn of a new day. I realized that inside even the seemingly worst circumstances, there is always a pathway home to one's Self and greater inner freedom. I began to expand my use of *up until now* and *from this point forward*. I used them to tell myself deeper truths about my feelings and fears. I began to say things like, Up until now, *when I don't understand things, I feel vulnerable and at risk; but* from this point forward, *I will accept life as it comes and trust the capability and resilience of my Self.*

Through these deeper truths I got to see subtle ways that "forever" lived in my life and controlled me. The more I applied *up until now* and *from this point forward*, the more resilient, capable, and free I became.

* * *

Maybe a year after I started applying *up until now* and *from this point forward* to my relationship with Steve, I was in a weekend workshop. The subject was reframing our pain as being lessons for compassion and understanding. Here's what came to me regarding my brother:

There is no such thing as a wasted LIFE. LIFE is so much bigger than my small purview. My brother's life is bumping into LIFE and creating more LIFE. I trust that LIFE can take care of itself in my brother's hands. I trust LIFE has use for Steve. In truth, LIFE is not unhappy one bit being expressed through Steve. LIFE aims to express. Steve is as perfect a place of expression as any I know or have seen. LIFE accepts Steve as its portal and SO DO I. Steve's life teaches me to look and love beyond the surface. His life teaches me to experience life's sometimes painful complexity and still see the good. Steve's life reminds me that everyone is multifaceted—each of us is dark and light, strong and insecure, capable and lost, and through it all, LIFE through LOVE is compassionate, understanding, and profoundly protective and accommodating. Steve teaches me to love him by wanting the best for him and by accepting him as he is. Thank you, Steve, for the wisdom you bring to my life.

The shift in my experience of my brother and my new respect for his life and choices were profound. I was blessed to love Steve without judgment or fear for three full years before he died.

In a family session during Steve's last stay at rehab, I had the opportunity to read to him my reframing of our relationship. He cried. He then shared it with every struggling person in the rehab center.

The idea that we will have to live with a pain forever is a lie.

The idea that "there's nothing we can do" about something is also a lie: *We can change! The way we see life and judge ourselves can change. We can open a door and invite in new perspectives and with them new possibilities. We can decide to be happy and fulfilled . . . no matter what!*

The excitement this realization and sense of possibility ignited in me grew exponentially when I read that science has discovered that the brain is capable of change throughout our entire lives. New thoughts and experiences can rewire old programming. We *can* teach an old dog new tricks. This news gives us all license to challenge every old issue and knock them down one by one.

The only "forever" worthy of our time is this truth: *From this point forward*, our lives are *forever available* to new perspectives and possibilities.

Inner Fitness Practice

The Big Lie

Some pain lasts forever.

The Truth

The only "forever" worthy of your time is this: *From this point forward*, your life is *forever* available to new perspectives and possibilities.

The Possibility

Knowing that every hurt, drama, trauma, upset, disappointment, and fear, no matter how deeply felt and no matter how long you have lived with it, can change for the better.

Try This

1. Set the intention right now that you will catch yourself—that is, suddenly become aware of what you are saying or doing—when you hear your surviving self taking the same old stance, engaging the same old beliefs, or seeing in the same old ways.

2. Stop yourself in mid-sentence or mid-thought when the unwanted, habitual way of thinking or speaking surfaces. Rethink and restate using the phrases *up until now* and *from this point forward:* Up until now I have habitually seen or done things this way, but from this point forward I can have a more authentic experience of my Self.

3. Keep coming back to this mindset. Practice shifting to the thriving mindset that *freedom is possible.*

Look and you will see that underneath "forever" thinking lives the idea that something is wrong . . . or against you.

Are You Living Life Thinking Something's Wrong or Against You?

The truth is, there is nothing wrong with our lives.
Life is showing up the way life shows up.

I WAS SITTING IN ONE OF MY FAVORITE RESTAURANTS, computer out, writing, focused, and finding my way into a story. Out of the corner of my eye I saw a man at the next table lean to his left and bend toward the floor to fiddle with his shoe. The woman sitting with him could not tell what he was doing. She suddenly became more erect and asked, "What's wrong?" He shook his head and explained something about his shoe. I didn't think about their exchange until I heard the question, "What's wrong?" asked twice more in a short span of time. *(When things happen in threes in my life, I take note.)*

Shortly after the couple's exchange, my waitress came to the table and saw my food untouched. This is unusual for me. I was a regular at the restaurant, and I ordered the tuna melt, every time. She poured me another round of iced tea, while eyeing my plate. Finally she asked, "Is something wrong with the sandwich?" "No," I said, "Just trying to get a thought that's in my head down on paper first." She smiled and moved on. Again, I paid this exchange no attention.

Ten minutes later I went to the ladies' room. Both stalls were taken, and it seemed that the occupants were friends. As one exited her stall and went to the sink, it sounded like the woman in the other stall dropped something. The friend at the sink looked up into the mirror, focusing on the reflection of her friend's stall door, and asked, "What's wrong?"

That last "What's wrong?" tied the three exchanges together, and I had a revelation: We human beings are conditioned to think in terms of what's *wrong*. On the surface this was not a profound revelation, but following this thought would lead me to profound personal discoveries.

These three exchanges in context made sense. But in my mind, I questioned, *Why did each person ask, "What's wrong?"* The woman in the restaurant could have asked the man, "What's going on?" The waitress might have asked, "Are you unhappy with your sandwich today?" And the friend in the bathroom could have easily said, "Are you okay?" But the words each used were, "What's wrong?" Something we all say often. That's when my awareness began to form about what I call *something's wrong or against me* thinking.

I've coined this phrase—*something's wrong or against me* thinking—as an inner fitness tool. It helps us to see the unconscious tendency we human beings have to think that something's either wrong or actively against us. Take note and I am certain you will find that often when you encounter an unfamiliar or confusing circumstance, you think that something's wrong with the situation, something's wrong with you, or even, dare I say, something's wrong with God and the way life works. Becoming aware of this knee-jerk reaction makes it possible for us to challenge it.

On the short walk from the restaurant bathroom back to my table, my mind flipped through a million scenarios. Like how, when the phone rings late at night, *What's wrong?* is my first thought; how when someone I love does something unusual, or looks at me in an unusual way, I react with a concerned *What's wrong?* I remember my mother saying once that when she passes a stalled car or accident her knee-jerk thought is, *I hope that's not one of my kids.*

As I returned to my table and settled into my seat, I settled into my conclusion that we human beings are primed to think that something's wrong or against us. As I ate my sandwich and mulled on this thought, I tried to challenge this conclusion and find it flawed.

* * *

I see myself as a positive person. Ask anyone. I am quick to see possibility. I look through rose-colored glasses, and I always hope for the best. Some people have called me annoyingly positive. I can find even the most obscured silver lining. I like this about myself.

I did not like the idea that in the recesses of my positive mind I was actually thinking about *what's wrong*. But the *I feel something's wrong or against me* revelation was tenacious. I kept seeing scenarios—mine and those drawn from conversations with others—that seemed to say that this *I feel something's wrong or against me* thought was worth exploring, despite my desire to see myself as "above" such thinking. *(I have learned that if I don't want to look at something, it's probably something I need to look at.)* The following day I was given proof that the *I feel something's wrong or against me* tendency was alive and well inside of me.

I was driving from the hair salon in Culver City through Hollywood, headed to my home in Los Feliz. I've been using Highland Avenue to get through Hollywood for thirty years. It's the fastest route and takes about thirty minutes.

It's also an easy route to slip into that automatic pilot trance where you turn the car on, buckle yourself in, and then drive—and before you know it you arrive at your destination. But you don't have any memory of the drive. You drove without thinking. Or, as I found on this particular drive, the better statement is, I drove most of the way without being aware of the thoughts that were thinking *themselves* in my mind.

I had driven twenty minutes and was at a red light along the Hollywood Bowl corridor, ten minutes from my home. I suddenly became aware of myself sitting at the light. When I realized I had driven the whole way mostly unconsciously, I took stock of myself. I noticed that my mind had been grinding on a thought for blocks. I focused on my thinking, trying to clearly see the thought that had been keeping me company for at least ten minutes.

I discovered that I had been busy telling someone off. I say "someone" because there was no particular person I was arguing with. There was no real-life axe I was grinding, no real transgression to be addressed. It was a fantasy argument, conjured up by my mind for no particular reason, except to maybe be at war with something for sport.

I felt excited, because I had read that the reptilian part of our brain is always on the lookout for danger. Was this evidence of the propensity of that part of our brain to skip over the good and zero in on the one thing that could possibly be, or become, a problem . . . even if that thing was a decades-old argument or fantasy? In the absence of any clear and present danger, do we rummage through our mental files and create "something's wrong" scenarios?

Here I was, totally engaged in a made-up conflict, coming up with "comebacks" should this or that happen. I thought about it and determined I had been occupied with this unprovoked drama for at least twenty blocks, maybe longer!

I wondered how often this happens. *How often am I unconsciously fighting a fight, or creating fantasy fights? How often am I using my mind in other unproductive ways?* Why would my brain choose to think about an old or made-up infraction that had no immediate relevance to my life? I could be using that "war time" to think about my goals and what is possible for my life, or to reminisce on my successes or my very real sense of gratitude. But instead, here I was hypnotized by "something's wrong" thinking.

I don't believe in coincidences, so I took note of the invisible war going on inside of me. I remembered that just the day before, at the restaurant, I had been unsure whether *something's wrong or against me* thinking even lived in me, because, as I said, I am such a positive person. But now I could not deny it. I had just caught my unconscious mind grinding away, engaged in war.

At that stoplight, one of my favorite inner fitness exercises for building Self-awareness was birthed. Expanding our awareness of our thinking and behavior is both a core aim and a benefit of pursuing inner fitness. I decided to turn my life into a research study and to use stop signs to help me become aware of the unconscious thoughts that hijack my attention. I taught myself to check in with myself every time I encounter a stop sign—to become aware of the thoughts I had been thinking during my drive and when necessary refocus my thinking. I chose stop signs as opposed to stoplights because I encountered stop signs less frequently. This meant I could drive for stretches

probably unconscious and encounter stop signs without antic-
ipating them. This would give me a better chance to actually
glimpse my unconscious mind at work. I wanted to see how
I was allowing my mind to work, and if I didn't like what I
found, I would take charge of my thoughts.

My mother and father had often warned me and my siblings
that if we did not think for ourselves, others would happily step
in and think for us. They never said anything about negative
fantasies being happy to take over my thinking, but I knew
this *something's wrong or against me* thinking qualified. It was
establishing a habit and tone of thinking that I did not wish
for my life. I did not wish to live my life constantly fighting
with something or somebody. I did not wish to interpret life or
the behaviors of others as being against me. I did not want to
randomly worry.

When I woke up at the Hollywood Bowl stoplight, I felt a
slight tension in my shoulders. My stomach had a slight knot
in it—like the feeling I have in my gut when I am preparing
for bad news. Without a doubt I was experiencing firsthand the
connection between my random fantasy argument and feelings
of stress. Again, I wondered, *How often does this happen?*

Stressful thoughts flood our nervous systems with stressful
feelings. Research says this happens because the mind does not
know how to distinguish between what is real and what is only
imagined. To the mind, it's all the same. Fantasy stress impacts
the nervous system just like real stress. In the same way we can
wake from a dream in a sweaty-palm panic, the thoughts that

circulate in our minds affect us—positively or negatively.

If my revelation was right, and we human beings are primed to think *something's wrong or against us*, then this could be part of the reason why so many people are stressed out. We are literally living life unconsciously waiting for that traumatic event that will leave us devastated.

This thought that we humans live much of life in fear of encountering devastation struck a chord. I had to admit that this fear lived in me. It lived as the prayer that something wouldn't suddenly sweep into my life and leave me feeling lost, devastated, or worse—annihilated.

With this thought came images of our prehistoric ancestors. I imagined in my mind's eye how afraid they must have been. We know and understand today so much that our ancestors didn't, such as the earth is round, not flat, and you can't fall off. Or how to survive and prepare for disasters like earthquakes, tornadoes, brush fires, or floods. I imagined the internal stress these ancestors felt. They had to be ready to fight or run from all kinds of dangers—wild animals or violent bands of other people.

Today, we know that the nervous system, in support of our safety, is programmed to fight, flee, or freeze in the face of danger. This is essentially the same nervous system that was programmed in our ancestors for dealing with the dangers all around them. So these nervous tendencies and fears have been handed off to us and condition us to look for and prepare for the worst.

We no longer have to fight off wild animals and clans of enemies, but sitting at that stoplight, I realized I was nonetheless prepared and ready to fight.

At that moment I designed an inner fitness observation exercise and committed to doing it for one day: I gave myself the assignment to "observe" how often I behave or react as though something's wrong, or how often I think something is against me. I am still practicing this exercise years later.

***

Self-observing is a great skill to practice. I learned it at a weekend personal development course conducted at Esalen, a retreat center along the California coast. The weekend experience was life-changing in so many wonderful ways that years later I now conduct my own inner fitness retreats to share tools for navigating life.

To Self-observe, we must first climb into our *observer's chair* with the intention of catching sight of our surviving self in action. The goal is to become aware of our unconscious, automatic behaviors, assumptions, and reactions.

Here's how using an observer's chair works: In your imagination, envision a chair positioned just above your right shoulder. My chair is the kind of director's chair you see on a movie set. The director sits in it and calls out "Action!" or "Cut!" as he or she directs the movie scenes. Whatever chair you imagine, when you climb into your observer's chair, you can clearly and objectively see your life, like watching a movie. *(Sometimes parts of my life are so fascinating I even envision myself with pop-corn in hand.)*

The benefit of climbing into our observer's chair is that it builds objective awareness of ourselves. Again, awareness is key. It is the first component necessary for understanding or changing anything. Like watching a movie, awareness allows us to see more of the picture and understand the bigger drama. When we can see our life, circumstances, behaviors, and beliefs, we can choose to keep things as they are or to change them.

Sitting in my observer's chair, I caught sight of a tendency I had to be defensive. It had been with me for years, but I assumed it was just "how I was." But the more I watched this tendency, the more I saw how it manipulated me—and how unnecessary it was.

Seeing this so clearly allowed me to stop reacting in the same old ways or drawing the same old *something's against me* conclusions. Awareness allowed me to opt out of the habit. We can't change what we can't see. The observer's chair helps us become conscious of the unconscious things we believe, do, say, or think.

Sitting in the observer's chair also provides the added benefit of experiencing upsets with a healthy distance between our Self and the events. We can experience challenges without having those challenges define us. Again, it's like watching a movie. We feel a character's pain and cry at the sad parts of a movie, but then we get up, leave the theater, and go on with our lives.

The first day I engaged this exercise, I was shocked at the number of unconscious fights I found myself in. I was at war all the time. Or I found myself sucking my teeth, rolling my eyes at this or that, and looking for someone to compare myself to or blame. And even if I am exaggerating a bit, what is not an exaggeration was how often the stop sign exercise revealed my *something's wrong or against me* thinking.

I have come to love stop signs—because they give me the opportunity to stop, breathe, take stock of my thinking, and reset my attitude and beliefs. Stop signs have taught me to shift away from *I feel something's wrong or against me* thinking and embrace the truth that I get to choose how I respond to people and events in my life. When I shift away from ideas of war, victimhood, and blame, I can think about what's possible for my life. I can thrive.

The truth is, there is nothing wrong with our lives. Life is showing up the way life shows up. Life never checks in with us to see whether there is a more convenient time for it to be life. The less I take life personally, and the more I develop a stronger inner Self, the more I know that with a little guidance and support, I can stand up to life. We all can. This is why I am so passionate about the importance of developing our inner fitness. Plenty of hurt comes with life. With a strong inner Self, however, it doesn't matter if things don't go the way we want, because we're good inside no matter what. This powerful truth makes *something's wrong or against me* a big fat lie.

After many years of practicing my stop sign exercise, I am

happy to say that more often than not I catch myself envisioning wonderfully rewarding scenarios. And when I catch myself snagged by surviving self thinking, I ask myself, *What would be the better, healthier thought? What thought would my thriving Self think?* And then, I think *that* thought.

What does *your* mind dwell on when you don't pay attention? Stop sign "therapy" takes work. But your life is worth it.

Inner Fitness Practice

The Big Lie

"I feel something's wrong or against me."

The Truth

You get to choose what you dwell on. The tone and quality of your thinking affect you physically and emotionally. Self-love requires that you be conscious of your thinking and choose responsible, loving thoughts that support Self-care.

The Possibility

Defaulting to thriving thoughts—thinking about what you want and what is possible for your life; allowing excitement to rise within you; being enthusiastic and curious; contemplating the truth that "God don't make junk"; and seeing problems as opportunities for you to grow and discover how capable and resilient you are.

Try This

1. Climb into your observer's chair and take note of everything.

2. Train yourself to shift your thinking when you find yourself in a negative thought loop.

Go to TinaLifford.com and download a free tool called the ASAL (*Ascending Scale to an AWESOME Life*). This will help you identify behaviors that belong to the surviving self and those that belong to the thriving Self and infinite SELF.

The biggest lie: the challenge you've been struggling with for so long you don't believe it can ever change.

Are You Bullied by an Old Sacred Torture?

The inner Self is forever poised to step over the quicksand of our greatest challenge and turn it into personal power.

I HATE IT WHEN PEOPLE TALK ABOUT LIFE LIKE IT'S A WALK in the park. It isn't. I hate it when people say, 'Just forget about that. Let it go.' How can people tell you to just 'forget about that' when they don't know what's in your bag?" These are the words the character Marsha says in my play *The Circle*, which is based on true stories.

We all know the bag Marsha is talking about. It is full of past hurtful events, the lies we've been unconsciously or maliciously told, and the lies we tell ourselves. In Marsha's bag is her memory of being five years old and raped by her uncle while her mother forbid her to resist. Marsha believes some things are so hurtful or devastating that we can't let go of them. This thought is a lie. I used to believe this lie, but I don't anymore.

Learning to separate ourselves from lies is the inner fitness journey.

My mother tells me I used to love to sing. I don't remember this, but I do remember when in the fifth grade I entered the school talent show. I was going to sing "Ole John Henry." I was excited. Then the morning of the talent show, while I was in gym class doing moves no one else could do on the trampoline, the performance roster for the talent show was handed out. I saw that my name was first on the list, and for some unexplainable reason I took a deep breath filled with fear. I uttered "Uh-oh" and every cell in my body seemed to go on alert. My heart went into a panic and stayed bunched in a knot the rest of the day. Throughout the morning, I carried that "uh-oh" knotted up inside of me. And then it followed me onto the stage that afternoon.

Two bars into the song I completely froze. Feelings of fear crawled up from my feet into my heart, and within seconds I was overwhelmed and paralyzed—stuck to one spot on the stage, unable to move or utter a note. After twenty-four bars of silence that should have been filled with my singing, my teacher, Mr. Hill, caught sight of my panic-stricken face. He ran to center stage, picked me up, and carried me to the wings.

I don't remember ever singing or humming, even around the house, after that.

For years, that moment of gulped fear lived in my cells. The humiliating embarrassment of Mr. Hill having to rescue me in front of the fully occupied auditorium burrowed deep inside of me. I had no idea that my intense sense of being overwhelmed rewired me in ways that would take years—decades—to undo.

That stage fright event receded into the folds of my brain. I went on to become an actress, but years later the stage fright memory was triggered again during an audition. The discomfort I felt was much like that of the talent show, and I found myself battling during the audition to stay present and not freeze.

* * *

I have accomplished many things beyond my acting career. More often than not, I do so as the confident girl on the trampoline, executing a complicated move by pushing my thinking mind out of the way and letting my body's intelligence take over. But that gulp of fear I took in the gym burdened me. A slight anxiety began to live alongside my career dreams. It was fear that the fifth-grade recurring memory overwhelm would show up again and that I would be left for days, weeks, or years trying to recover. The fear was at times so great I doubted I would ever be free of it.

For long stretches at a time this fear would seem to disappear. Then, when I least expected, it would grab hold of me again. I managed it by pitting my will against it. I used my success to distract me from the painful reality that no matter how confident I was in other areas, this area of challenge owned me . . . tortured me. (If the word *tortured* sounds intense, think about that experience in your life which haunts you, knots your stomach, makes you feel insecure and at its mercy, or that simply feels bigger than you.) I refer to such recurring memory overwhelm as a *sacred torture*: any event that happened in our lives that now convinces us through fear that it is more real and powerful than we are. It is sacred because, as you will see, we hold on to it in a way that, pray as we might, doesn't leave room for God or for the light of new possibilities to enter.

We all have or have had at least one sacred torture or area of challenge that has been a sore spot for longer than we want. When triggered, our sacred torture throws us into an unstable fearful state and we generally react irrationally. I call this a *crazy trauma drama moment*. Moments like these can be so intense that they seem to have a will all their own.

I can speak candidly about my crazy trauma drama because I came to see it as a lie. Dismantling that lie became the path down which I forged my inner fitness. I am proud of this. But to get myself free of the lie and dream a bigger dream, I knew I had to do something different. I had to learn to see myself and be with my Self in new ways. I had to observe my unconscious self in action, understand why I do the things I do, and interrupt my old reactions with new behavior.

I read books (like you are doing right now), enrolled in a

spiritual psychology program, attended self-help workshops, and found a great therapist. Information helped me to see and understand myself. I discovered that I wasn't flawed or broken or "less than." I was human. My pain was not unique. Hurts, dramas, traumas, upsets, disappointments, and fears are part of the human package along with everything else in life. The problem was not that I experienced hurt (that's human); the problem was that I was uninformed about how best to take care of myself when my sacred torture was triggered. I learned that *how* we think about challenges helps shape our experience of them. Understanding that emotions can "loop," creating a self-perpetuating experience, transformed how I interacted with my thoughts.

My stage fright experience was the perfect example of a self-perpetuating loop in action: I took that gulp of fear in gym class years ago, but that fear spawned thoughts about failing and experiencing embarrassment in front of an audience. This made me more afraid, which created more pictures of what I didn't want . . . and so on! Thus, I was caught in a fear loop. Between gym class and the talent show (and later, before many auditions), I battled with anxiety and contemplated strategies I could turn to if fear began to get the best of me. In other words, I spent hours with pictures and thoughts of failure running through my mind. Eventually, I came to see that adjusting for or battling with how I was going to be afraid simply fed the fear—I was programming myself for exactly what manifested. I now know that focusing on what I want—visualizing pictures and thoughts of the *desired* outcome—is a powerful tool that can help calm nerves and support success.

When we feel threatened, even if the threat is only perceived and not "real," an emotional loop can be triggered. The obvious problem with this function of our brains is that we relive over and over the very experiences we seek distance from. This loop can leave us feeling like there's no way out.

When it comes to our greatest challenges, we all would love to "just let it go." But almost every common strategy for getting distance from our discomfort—running from it, strong-arming it with will, even praying—when done out of fear, desperation, or a sense of losing the battle serves instead to hold the fear loop in place.

So it makes sense that some painful experiences feel too big to overcome. But it is this very thought that does the greatest damage because it tells us, *We can't change things, so why try?* Instead of envisioning freedom from an old hurt or painful memory, we are left to relentlessly manage it. Often, we hide our struggle from the world, pretending like we've got it all together.

* * *

The lie that harasses you probably has nothing to do with stage fright. But the feeling of being held hostage by an old sacred torture or recurring memory, and the desire to be free of its overwhelm, even as you doubt such freedom is possible, might be familiar.

The belief that an emotional pain is bigger than the inner Self is one of the biggest, most challenging and damaging LIES—false statements—of all.

I had pretty much thrown up my hands at the idea of ever being free of my fifth-grade sacred torture. But the thriving Self, whose nature is forever optimistic and focuses on what's possible, would not allow me to give up hope of being on the other side of this challenge. It kept whispering, *If anyone has ever gotten over a great challenge, then it is possible for everyone— including you.* What a thought! It makes sense.

The inner Self is forever poised to step over the quicksand of our greatest challenge and turn it into personal power.

One of my most empowering inner fitness realizations came when I read that the brain is never fixed. IT CAN CHANGE AT ANY AGE. This means that old pain can change. A new experience is possible. There is hope. We are not doomed to be ruled by our hurts, dramas, traumas, upsets, disappoint- ments, and fears. When lies crash into our lives and leave us with bruises, lumps, or tears, the unscathed infinite SELF still exists underneath these events. It is our job to dig through the debris and reconnect with our Self.

* * *

Interacting with a sacred torture in new ways is the path to rewiring, healing, and reconnecting us to our Self. *From this point forward*, as you start to experience old recurring memory overwhelm, say to yourself, *Respond differently this time.* Start by imagining the unscathed Self—the infinite SELF that is as ancient and resilient as life itself and lives inside of you, waiting to support you.

Practice acknowledging this Self and believing that it is more powerful than the scars left by hurts, dramas, traumas, upsets, disappointments, and fears. Remind yourself that the surviving self resists change even when it is good for us. It will use our discomfort to get us to abort our efforts to change.

When old emotions bubble up, instead of reacting, tell yourself to slow down, get still. Watch yourself in action; see your fear and confusion; allow yourself to feel the discomfort that forms in your heart and body. Doing so won't kill you, no matter what your old habit of fear tells you. Doing so will strengthen you. It will teach you that your boogeyman lies to you. Talk to yourself the way you would to a child who does not yet know that the boogeyman is not real. Breathe through the moment instead of getting caught up in the drama of it. Say out loud, *No matter how painful or dramatic this feels, no matter how long this has challenged me up until now, I am bigger than this. My life is more than this issue, more than the moment that created it. My fears are mis-wired, confused emotions that can right themselves the more I breathe through them and talk to my Self, telling my Self higher truths.*

When we begin to alter our response to a painful pattern in even the slightest of ways, the new response weakens the old pattern. The more we meet an old pattern with new internal behavior, the more the old pattern is disrupted and destabilized. Until one day, it no longer controls us. Such effort teaches us to ignore our old thoughts and makes room for us to engage and strengthen our inner Self. This is how our most challenging, oldest lies unravel and die and new, more rewarding possibilities are born.

***

One day, and countless self-help books later, I stopped resisting or dreading a sacred torture incident. When one did occur, I did not allow my mind to turn the moment into a "forever" state, nor did I let it convince me that "something was wrong" or that I was broken in some way that needed to be fixed. I accepted that my reactions were connected to old wiring. Knowing this lessened the reactions and their control over me. It helped me to stop habitually judging myself and jumping to negative conclusions—feeling like I had backslid and not made any real progress. I could feel nervousness and be disconnected from it at the same time, not take it seriously or personally, not make it mean something that induced fear or shame.

These efforts strengthened my Self. I began to feel more powerful than my surviving self. I began to believe that I was not alone in this big world: I was connected to an intelligent force that cares. Its nature was a part of me. It was as if the force had invited me to a big party called life. My name was on the guest list: I mattered.

These were just concepts at first. But as I struggled to see from this point of view and respond differently to my challenges, faith was forged. My moment-to-moment choice regarding old patterns and fear was clear: either aim to trust that there is a part of me that can thrive no matter the pain or circumstance, or continue to be afraid and forever controlled by hurt and fear.

* * *

Putting all that I was learning into action was key. In the midst of a triggered moment, instead of battling with memory overwhelm, I asked myself, *Do I believe this challenge is bigger than God?* The answer was always "No." **What good is a belief system if it is not more powerful than the challenges we face?** When logic can poke holes in our sacred torture, it's just a matter of time before the entire lie unravels.

This next question I asked opened my eyes and transformed my life: *On a scale of 1 to 10, with 10 being "I've totally turned the problem over to my higher power," where was I in turning my stage fright over to God?* (Use whatever term you like, but *God* to me is that infinite SELF inside of us that is bigger than our small ideas of ourselves, and bigger than any lie. It is the starting point for new possibilities. It is the truth that no lie can upstage.)

When I asked myself that question, the answer "2" popped into my head, clear as day. I was shocked. That number meant that I hadn't come close to handing anything over to God. How was this possible—with all the prayers I had prayed and all the inner work I had done trying to rid myself of this challenge?

I had prayed when getting dressed for auditions and whenever intense nervousness surfaced; I had prayed in bed at night, asking for support; I had prayed for and envisioned rock-solid inner confidence; I had prayed through tears and deep sadness and embarrassment; and I had prayed before and after visits to the therapist, hypnotist, and energy healers. I had prayed over and over. Where the hell did this "2" come from?

Then I saw the truth. Yes. There *was* a lot of "Oh God, I want you to fix this, change this, and help me move beyond this." But when I checked inside of myself using a scale of 1 to 10, the truth was revealed: I felt all but defeated. Stage fright had been problematic for me for so long that I couldn't imagine that the seas might part and I'd be able to cross into freedom. Instead, I shrank in the shadow of my sacred torture where I feared I would remain forever small and afraid. At that moment I realized that I had prayed without believing that freedom was possible.

I came to realize that even my prayers were intimidated by my fear. That's when the idea of the "sacred" torture first came to me.

* * *

Anything and everything can qualify as a sacred torture. An actress client who had battled acne since she was a teenager told me: "I used to pray for clear skin, but I've had this problem for so long, I've given up. There's no hope left. I know I'm always going to have this skin problem."

I asked her to check inside of herself and tell me whether deep inside she had left any room for God and other possibilities. To her surprise, her answer was "no." She had ceased to hope—"there's no hope left."

Change can't happen without an opening through which it can enter.

Acne was this client's sacred torture. Yet through our work together, she discovered that waiting deep inside of her was the part that was untouched by acne—the part in each of us that is never hurt, harmed, or endangered by the lies we carry.

I ran into this client some time later, and her skin was glowing. She had found a great doctor and changed her diet. I smiled. These answers were always there waiting for her to reach past her old doubt toward new possibility.

* * *

Lies blind us, leaving us unable to see them clearly. And if we can't see them, we can't dismantle them.

Telltale signs let us know when we are dealing with a sacred torture: feelings of hopelessness, Self-rejection, and harsh Self-criticism; a sense of shame that makes us feel we must hide our experience from the world. Such signs indicate that somewhere in our lives someone said something to us, or we had an experience, that crashed into our sense of ourselves and safety. We are left with the lie that we are damaged, small, and powerless. When we hold on to our chronic troubling issues, with no sense of possibility, we buy the lies that these issues tell.

You are more than the biggest lie that's ever made its way into your life. This is not an affirmation. This is a truth, and it can be your starting point to freedom: *If you are made by the same intelligent force that created the universe, then inside your nature is the power you need to move beyond any and every lie that has ever hurt you.* You must let the truth of this statement pull you upward. Contemplate a new possibility. Rebuild your relationship with your Self. And reveal your inner power and wholeness.

The idea that there must be a way out of pain is a clear, rational, and necessary thought, worthy of deep consideration. The trick is to commit to this idea. Hold on to it tightly, especially when an old sacred torture is triggered and you doubt you will ever know freedom from it.

From this point forward, when you think you've turned a lie over to your higher power, use a scale from 1 to 10 to check inside. The truth will always be revealed. **Assigning a number from 1 to 10 to everything important will reveal where you are, and the information you gain can send you in the direction of where you want to go.**

Let's go back to Marsha's question from my play *The Circle*—"How can people tell you to just 'forget about that' when they don't know what's in your bag?" The answer? We learn to forget about it when we decide once and for all there is an answer to what troubles us. Do not waver on this. Then, from within, you'll be led to the people, books (like this one), and inner fitness practices that make the difference you seek. Knowing there is an answer to your sacred torture will pull to the surface the freedom that is inside you waiting to become your new way of life.

Inner Fitness Practice

The Big Lie

Your greatest challenge in life is bigger and stronger than you.

The Truth

You are more than the biggest lie that's ever made its way into your life.

The Possibility

Moving beyond your greatest challenge and the stress it causes. Having tools to help you manage a sacred torture or any recurring memory overwhelm more effectively.

Try This

1. Become aware of when you are being triggered by an old hurt, drama, trauma, upset, disappointment, or fear.

2. Remind yourself to courageously respond differently than you have responded in the past— no matter how small that response might be.

3. Rate, on a scale from 1 to 10, the degree to which you feel change is possible; then rate the degree to which you've turned your challenge over to a higher power. This will give you a concrete picture of your unconscious feelings and thoughts.

4. When you see where you are, decide where you want to be and create a thought strategy, or reframe, for moving forward. (*Reframe* means restating your thought in an empowering way. For instance, if your sacred torture makes you feel stupid, a reframe might be: *Up until now, I have felt stupid, but the truth is there is a brilliant part of me that knows many things, and what I don't know I can ask for help with and learn.*)

Knowing that freedom is possible encourages the next step, and the one that follows.

Are You Tired of Being Knocked Off Your Center by That Old Pattern?

Man can find every truth connected with his being
if he will dig deep into the mine of his soul.

—JAMES ALLEN, "AS A MAN THINKETH"

I BEGAN TO DISMANTLE MY SACRED TORTURE BACK IN the early 1990s one fateful night while hanging out on the Santa Monica Pier. Back then, numerous burger and beer joints and a wonderful health food eatery broke up the long row of funky little shops selling tie-dyed T-shirts, incense, and posters.

I was hanging out with my friend Nirvana. This self-chosen name was a definite sign of the times. The crowd I hung out with was looking for nirvana—that state in spiritual development where one becomes free of suffering. How appropriate that one of my greatest inner fitness lessons related to suffering happened in the company of my friend Nirvana.

We were walking past a shop, and I was drawn to a provocative poster in the window by Richard Avedon showing the actress Nastassja Kinski lying nude and intertwined with a Burmese python. It was a fascinating photo, and I gazed at it for maybe five minutes. Taking it in. I locked in on every component of its composition. I particularly liked the pops of color. The proximity of the snake's red tongue to her ear made me stick my baby finger in my left ear and wiggle free of the willies that had crawled in.

Then I noticed that a small crowd had gathered in front of another poster. One of the gazers asked her friend, "Can you see it?" Everyone was tilting his or her head from one side to the other, clearly trying to find the "right" position. Another person excitedly said, "I see it!" Then another, "I'm in!"

Nirvana was part of the staring crowd. "What are they looking at?" I asked. He explained that "hidden" in the 2-D poster of a Paris street scene was a detailed 3-D experience of the same scene. If you looked at the scene long enough, from the right perspective, the flat, 2-D image literally "popped" into an intricate 3-D image. I looked at the not-so-special 2-D poster, and it was hard to believe that simply by staring at it, a whole other world could pop into view. But Nirvana had seen it.

After I had spent a few minutes tilting my head from one side to the other, grumbling, he reassured me, "It's there. Keep looking." I returned to the poster with fierce focus . . . nothing. I moved closer to the poster, hoping that would help me see what everyone else could see. Nothing. I backed away from it . . . still nothing.

I am a competitive spirit at heart. I was determined to stand there looking at that poster FOREVER if I had to. If other people were able to see this fascinating 3-D world, then I was not going home until I had joined their club.

Then it happened. Suddenly, for a flash, the 3-D world popped into view. Only for a second or two, but I saw it long enough to know that what the others were saying was true.

Those two seconds were not enough for me to feel satisfied and head home, however. I planted my feet and looked at the poster again, telling myself to surrender because I had no idea how to *make* it happen. But this time, as I looked at the poster I had no doubt about the intricate world that was hidden in that piece of paper. I knew it was real. This time, when I looked at the Paris scene, I did so *knowing* it would become three-dimensional.

And it did. Soon after I began to look, the 3-D world popped up again, and this time it stayed for a longer time. I stared at it in rapt fascination, more absorbed than I had been observing every detail of the Nastassja Kinski poster.

I don't remember my drive home once Nirvana and I said goodbye. I was inside the world of that 3-D poster, walking its streets past shops and turning down corners. It was so real. I was mesmerized by how detailed the 3-D version of the poster was and how quickly one minute it was there and the next minute it had vanished from view. One blink, and the 3-D image could become a simple flat poster again.

Each time I lost the 3-D perception, it took a while to find my way back in. Reentry was not a science. There were no guaranteed steps to follow. But each reentry took less and less time, and I could hold on to the 3-D scene longer and longer. I can say that seeing the 3-D scene was enabled, at least in part, by a shift in my perception of the poster. From the moment I saw other people in front of that poster talking about something I could not see, my perception of life in general widened. I believed in a world I couldn't see. I trusted my ability to enter it. The more glimpses I caught of that 3-D world, the more I looked for it and expected to see it.

I became so committed to the 3-D image that I could not look at the 2-D poster as I had before. I knew it did not represent the whole truth. It was limited.

Of course, this is a metaphor for spiritual awakening. Spiritual teachers throughout the ages from Jesus and Buddha to modern-day enlightened thinkers like Michael Beckwith, Joe Dispenza, and Ken Wilber tell us there's a bigger reality behind the world we see and that our problems and challenges are a matter of perception. Shift our perception, and we can literally change our world. Also, like with the poster, once you have caught a glimpse of the spiritual world that the physical world sits in, you cannot look at the physical world in the same old way.

But this profound spiritual metaphor was not my most important lesson that night on the Santa Monica Pier: I began to see my *sacred torture* like I saw the 2-D poster—present, but not the truth.

* * *

The habit of seeing life through the lens of our sacred torture conditions us to see ourselves in the same limited (two-dimensional) ways. We come to expect, and make room for, the fear or discomfort associated with our sacred torture. For example, if we are used to feeling a certain anxiety, or queasiness in the stomach, or stress somewhere else in the body, the two-dimensional perception has us habitually expecting that experience whenever we encounter similar situations. We automatically define our experience in the same old way; and when an issue is not actively harassing us, we often go looking for it.

Take note of how, during stressful times, you wake up feeling just fine, free of any burdens, and then all of a sudden you remember that you're "supposed" to be worried. You literally wonder *Where is my worry?* as if it's lost and you're trying to find it. On cue, worry and stress drop right back in. Sri Ramana Maharshi, considered one of the most significant spiritual teachers to emerge from India, explains that when we first awaken from sleep, unconscious of burdens, we awaken as our real Self.

The 3-D version of the Paris poster represents the Self—intricately detailed yet seen only by those willing to challenge the reality of the 2-D world. Like the poster, we lose sight of our 3-D image—our Self—and the two-dimensional world of fear, worry, survival, and judgment grabs hold of us and pulls us in.

Our sacred torture wins because we have not learned to look at it long enough with calm to see through it to the other side. Our sacred torture makes us uncomfortable, so we run from that discomfort. We are so busy running from our discomfort that it winds up dictating our lives—such as a person who is afraid of elevators going only to places that have escalators. Our sacred torture tells us how we feel and which people and conversations are "safe."

The more effective choice is to challenge the discomfort by looking right at it—for as long as it takes. When I stood before the 2-D poster that night, I was determined. I was willing to stay there for as long as it took to see the 3-D world the others knew. Standing there, I perceived that the 2-D world was not a fixed reality—and neither is my sacred torture. Inside every sacred torture is a 3-D version of it waiting to be seen. Standing in front of our sacred torture and observing it, determined to see it morph, is a way to begin to dismantle its control over our lives.

That night I put my sacred torture on notice that I was ready to believe in a reality greater than it. I began to look at the old torture, fully expecting it to transform. And *from that point forward*, I had to practice my resolve over and over again. I made the pact with my Self that whenever I started to forget that I am more powerful than my challenges, something would happen to remind me . . . and something always did (and still does). This made me feel like the universe was listening to me and had my back.

I got into the habit of no longer seeing my challenges and fears as fixed "forever" states. When the habit of thinking in my old way surfaced, I would literally shake my head "no" and correct my thinking. Over time I began to see my challenges as overindulged thoughts in need of correction. I began to give those old challenges less attention. Instead, I allowed myself to contemplate freedom from any burden.

Here are steps you can take to begin your journey to freedom from your two-dimensional world:

1. Replace the idea that your sacred torture is more powerful than you are with the idea that you can be on the other side of its chronic pain. This thought is crucial. You must begin to leave room for the belief that freedom from your sacred torture is possible.

2. Use the experience of others to help build belief in this possibility. I dared to believe in something I could not see because my friend Nirvana and some other random people

said they had experienced it. Many spiritual teachers have said we are bigger than our challenges. I now know this is true. You can choose to trust your experiences and begin right now to ask your inner Self to please show you how to move beyond your sacred torture.

3. Stand in front of your 2-D challenge in spite of your discomfort. Even though it may be uncomfortable to look at and feel its pain, stand steadfast in that pain and discomfort anyway. This is the road to freedom. You must have faith that if you stand firm through the discomfort, at some point that picture will change and give you your 3-D view of things.

4. Take note of what you normally do when your sacred torture is triggered. Do you lash out, become despondent, eat, drink, cry, have sex? When this pattern is triggered, do something—even the smallest thing—differently. It doesn't take a lot to make just one adjustment. One new behavior you can try in such times is to ask yourself this question: *Am I looking at a 2-D picture? If so, what might the 3-D version look like?* This simple question challenges the 2-D habit and pulls your awareness to higher ground.

5. Enroll in workshops that focus on inner fitness techniques. Have conversations with people who you know have traveled the path you want to travel. *(You are welcome to hang out with me on Instagram or visit my website and attend my events.)*

6. A fantastic tool for rewiring the jammed emotional loop is
   called EFT, Emotional Freedom Technique, developed by
   Gary Craig. Google it. EFT calms the emotional reaction.
   It will help you face old situations without feeling habitual
   emotional overwhelm.

* * *

A therapist once told me that when we're being chased in a
dream, we should stop and turn around and look at what is
chasing us. This advice is counterintuitive to how we usually
deal with threatening things. We run. But when we can stop
and let all the feelings we are running from catch up to us, this
bold action dissolves the scary picture, changes the perspective,
and drains the power out of the thing that's been chasing us.

Throughout the ages spiritual teachers have taught that reality shifts when we shift our perspective. That evening on the
Santa Monica Pier, watching the poster image change from
2-D to 3-D, I came to see the 2-D picture—and any sacred
torture—as yet another subtle distracting lie—a falsehood—
that tries to control our sense of who we are. This realization
was so clear that for the first time in my life I knew, beyond
the shadow of a doubt, that a shift in perspective regarding any
issue is possible.

* * *

Your sacred torture is a lie. Dismantling it is possible. Decon-
struction starts by being courageous. Get to know your Self.

Then stand in front of your burdens centered in your Self, and tell your small surviving self the truth:

> I am bigger than your small idea of me. I expect freedom. I will stand here for as long as it takes.

Inner Fitness Practice

The Big Lie

The two-dimensional world is all there is.

The Truth

There is more to life than what you can see. When you stretch to *see* more, that effort changes everything.

The Possibility

Seeing your life in bold detail and discovering new possibilities and power that are already living inside of you.

Try This

When it comes to dismantling your sacred torture, do not run from it or be indulgent of it.

1. Interrupt the energy flow to those old memories and reactions as quickly as possible. For example, stop thinking the thought that is causing you distress. Don't avoid, however. Your job is to see the pattern and say: *I see you. I'm not going down that same old habitual road with you today.* The point here is to recognize the pairing between patterns and

feelings and do whatever you can to create distance between that old pairing. This will create room for a new experience.

2. Substitute defeatist thinking with empowering thoughts of what is possible. Think about what you want and where you want to go. (Examples: *I want to walk into rooms and add authentic value, feel comfortable in my skin. I want a relationship with someone I can communicate with like we are best friends. I want to be excited about other people's accomplishments. I want to be kind and respectful even when I feel afraid or uncomfortable.*)

3. Use the *up until now* and *from this point forward* tool (see Question 1).

4. Learn a system for defusing the energy in your sacred torture. I have had great success with EFT. (Again, Google it. You can learn the technique online for free.)

Standing up to old patterns lets every cell in your body know that you matter to your Self.

Do You Think That How You Feel Doesn't Matter?

Never ignore a person who loves you,
and misses you . . . especially if
that person is your Self.

W HAT DO THE GREAT LOVE AFFAIRS OF ROMEO AND Juliet, Richard Burton and Elizabeth Taylor, and Whitney Houston and Bobby Brown have in common with us? They are famous, and even infamous, examples of an all-consuming passion we all have experienced . . . if only in the privacy of our minds. We know that moment in our pasts when our hearts were full to bursting with love for someone. It didn't matter whether the person was right for us, or whether the person even knew we were alive. We were caught up in that glorious feeling we call love. What happens in these love highs however does matter. They can bring us great joy, or they can hand us a big fat lie that sets a choppy course for our lives.

In the fifth grade I was crazy about Jeffrey Alexander, who lived with his parents in a duplex downstairs from my girl-friend Debbie Smith. I talked to Debbie ad nauseam about Jeffrey. I told her how beautiful his eyes were, how his eyeglasses meant he was smart, and how much I liked his smooth Hershey's chocolate skin.

One day, when I was walking to school with Debbie and Jeffrey, he professed his undying love for me. I did one of those "You talking to me?" double takes, and then broke into a huge smile. Debbie smiled, too. She knew his words were my dream come true. Jeffrey and I walked together to and from school that day, holding hands.

The next day our fifth-grade love was the same. Then, just before the three o'clock bell rang, Jeffrey, who was seated right behind me next to Debbie, leaned forward and whispered: "I don't really love you. I never did. Debbie dared me to say it. Psych." I glanced at Debbie, whose eyes seemed to twinkle with self-satisfaction. I was blindsided by their mean joke. They had lied to me about the most important thing in my ten-year-old life. Why would my friends do such a thing?

Then I turned around, and they were both laughing. I felt a sting that went deep. Unbeknownst to me, a damaging lie had just made its way into my life. It would take me years to see it, and even more years to rewire it. I'm not just talking about the lie Jeffrey and Debbie cooked up on a dare. Of course, that hurt. But their lie birthed two other lies that marked me:

1. Love ends suddenly . . . every time.
2. My feelings don't matter.

This last lie I unknowingly told myself when I didn't speak up for myself and say to them: "Ouch! That joke wasn't funny! It was mean, and it hurt!" The idea that hurt doesn't matter is a lie. All hurts matter—even seemingly foolish childhood hurts—if we are left feeling diminished in any way.

It took two decades for me to see that Jeffrey's hurtful prank had actually created a "love" pattern in me. From that point, every relationship was the same: I would be crazy about a guy who wasn't crazy about me. Then, through some unexpected turn of events, I'd be blindsided by the sudden end of the relationship. This happened with Carl, Timothy, Mac, and Nathaniel. Yet I was oblivious to this relationship pattern.

When I look back, this pattern of sudden endings was so consistent in my dating life that there might as well have been a want ad tattooed to my forehead that read:

> **Wanted: Man who will appear to be perfect and then suddenly disappear.**

* * *

Too bad I didn't have a life skills class as part of my early education. Skills for navigating life would have been helpful. Instead, I was required to take home economics for two semesters in junior high school and learned to cook and sew. Today, I eat every meal out, and recently I paid $170 for a pair of jeans *with holes in them*.

A life skills class would have offered the kind of education a human being needs—instruction on how to sew our lives back together when hurts, dramas, traumas, upsets, disappointments, and fears come crashing in.

* * *

Jeffrey and Debbie left me flush with deeply felt embarrassment. I didn't have tools for navigating these feelings. I didn't know what behavioral scientists now know—that unresolved, highly charged emotions can control us unconsciously, can cause us to behave like puppets on a string. This is why knowledge of how our emotions and brains operate is important. Making inner fitness an aim equips us with this information and tools for navigating our tricky minds and emotional sensitivities.

Eckhart Tolle, in his watershed 1997 book *The Power of Now*, explains the phenomenon of how unresolved hurt "leaves behind a residue of pain that lives on in you" and turns into a pattern of pain, which he calls the pain-body:

> Every emotional pain that you experience leaves behind a residue of pain that lives on in you . . . This, of course, in-

cludes the pain you suffered as a child . . . If you look on it as an invisible entity in its own right, you are getting quite close to the truth . . . The pain-body wants to survive, just like every other entity in existence . . . It needs to get its "food" through you. It will feed on any experience that resonates with its own kind of energy, anything that creates further pain in whatever form: anger, destructiveness, hatred, grief, emotional drama, violence, and even illness . . . Its survival depends on your unconscious identification with it, as well as on your unconscious fear of facing the pain that lives in you. But if you don't face it, if you don't bring the light of your consciousness into the pain, you will be forced to relive it again and again.

Tolle is describing how our chronic emotional pain develops a life all its own inside of us. Through some kind of process that scientists do not yet understand, our chronic pain actively works to maintain itself. Once created, our pain-pattern (pain-body) fights to stay alive in us. The "food" it requires is more of the same kind of pain that created it.

The pain-body attracts people or circumstances, or creates situations that re-create the kind of pain and inner distur-bance it needs in order to stay alive: feeling betrayed or left out; feeling anger, grief, emotional drama, violence, illness. Like a vampire, our pain-patterns (pain-bodies) roam the dark places in our lives to find, or re-create, pain they can feed on. The more we identify with our old pain memories and experiences, the more food there is for the pain-body vampire to feed on.

I was forty years old when I read these words and saw my dating pain-body for the first time. My first reaction was to wish I had had this empowering information much earlier, but that thought just wasted more time. As I began to see my life more clearly, I learned that some lessons are better late than never.

One day, as I was reading this Tolle passage for the hundredth time, I made an unexpected discovery. The pain I felt with every sudden relationship breakup was the same pain I had felt that day when Debbie and Jeffrey played their mean joke on me. Everything was the same: my racing heart and feelings of shame, embarrassment, and isolation. During each breakup I fought back my tears and pretended that I didn't care—I didn't say "Ouch!" Though I always felt like the wind had been knocked out of me, I didn't say anything. I just moved on. This response was like a finely tuned orchestra playing the tragic opera *Suddenly in Pain, in B-Flat*, written by Jeffrey Alexander and me.

If by chance you can't relate to this particular story, then think about a memory or experience that has hung on in your life for a ridiculous number of years, creating its own pain-pattern.

Once I learned to look at my pain-pattern without being caught in it, there was space for a beautiful thought to cross my mind. What if I had handled that painful moment differently?

What if I had told Jeffrey and Debbie that their prank hurt my feelings, instead of brushing my feelings aside and pretending to be tough? Then, it hit me. The real and lasting pain from Jeffrey and Debbie was not their unkind act, but my own unconscious act—my unconscious rejection of my Self. My behavior sent a message to my Self that told me my feelings didn't matter.

* * *

Since that day when I didn't honor my feelings—didn't say "Ouch, that hurt!"—a part of me had been waiting to be seen, acknowledged, and reclaimed. I saw the ten-year-old me sitting at the door of my heart, feeling forgotten—like the last child at school who quietly sits in the main office waiting for his or her parent to show up. When I reviewed each sudden breakup, she was there—waiting, needing me, the most important person in her life, to speak up for her, to give her the love and attention she needed and deserved.

She longed for me to lovingly grab her in my arms, tell her I was sorry for not acknowledging her hurt, and say: *You did nothing wrong. I'm sorry I wasn't there for you.*

Could this be why our pain-patterns repeat? Does some rejected part of us need to be reclaimed, embraced, and loved before we can truly move on? I don't know. But I knew I needed to look the little girl in me in the eyes and tell her I was sorry and embrace her. So I did. I stood in front of my full-length mirror and looked myself in the eyes. I called forth my inner ten-year-old, replayed the Jeffrey and Debbie lie, and told my Self the truth: *You are lovable. I love you. I am sorry their behavior hurt you, and I am even sorrier that I didn't let you know back then how important and worthy you are. I will never, ever abandon you again.*

I stood there saying "I'm sorry" and tasted good tears. (If standing in front of a mirror in this way feels uncomfortable to you, find the expression of Self-acknowledgment that does feel good: Write your Self an apology letter, for instance, or create your own Self-forgiveness ritual.)

Hurtful things have happened to us all. For a myriad of reasons, we were not able to take care of ourselves. But it is never too late to give ourselves the care we need to move beyond the past.

The truth: Our feelings matter. They change us for the better or for the worse. We get better when we give our Self responsible, loving Self-care. We set ourselves up for chronic pain when we gloss over hurt like it doesn't matter.

Apologizing to our Self for ways we have mistreated, distrusted, or discounted our Self feels as good as hearing a deserved apology from a parent or friend. A simple Self-directed, heartfelt "I'm sorry" ignites healing. We may not be able to control the unkind acts of others, but we can choose to love our Self and feel worthy no matter what else is happening in our lives. When we ignore our feelings and don't give our Self the love of time and attention, we believe the big fat lie that

"We don't matter." The truth is, we *do* matter. Feelings matter. They deserve consideration. Feelings may not always tell us the truth, but they deserve to be considered.

The person inside of you is worthy. The person inside deserves your "I'm sorry." One sincere Self-directed "I'm sorry" might truly ignite the greatest love affair of all time.

Inner Fitness Practice

The Big Lie

You don't matter; your feelings don't matter.

The Truth

You *do* matter. Your feelings matter. It is your responsibility to address within yourself the moments you've glossed over that matter. You in a loving conversation with your Self supports healing.

The Possibility

Dissolving an old hurt and finally allowing it to heal through a heartfelt apology to your Self.

Try This

How you connect with the hurt part of you is up to you. You can choose to do one or all of the following, or make up your own Self-care healing experience.

1. Write your Self an apology.

2. Stand in front of a mirror, tell your Self that you love your Self, and apologize for a time when you treated your feelings like they didn't matter.

3. Without any blame or attack energy, let someone know how their behavior toward you feels to you. (Don't argue. Simply state what your experience is. An example might be, "When I'm speaking and you roll your eyes, I feel like you're devaluing my opinion.")

4. If your unspoken feelings involve someone deceased or unavailable, have a one-sided conversation with them and tell them how their actions and words felt to you. You can also write a letter to a deceased person and tell that person how you feel. Having someone read that message is not the point; acknowledging unaddressed hurt is.

When you know you matter,
you can tell your Self the truth
in ways that nurture Self-care.

What Does Your "I Can't" Really Mean?

I said yes, but I was just being nice.

T HE WINDOWS WERE FOGGY AND THE AIR JUST CHILLY enough to add to the excitement of having Jackson's tongue in my mouth and his hands trying to go where no man had gone before. I was sixteen, and Jackson was eighteen. A man. In the back seat of his green Taurus, I learned the truth that "I can't" is a lie.

I liked Jackson—a lot. I had been talking my then-best-friend Joyce's ear off for a year about all things Jackson: in hallways, between classes, "Joyce, look at the cool way he walks holding his head to one side!" In the schoolyard, "Joyce, Joyce, look at the way Jackson's friends wait to see how he responds before they respond!" On the telephone, "Joyce, last night I was talking to Jackson under the covers so my parents wouldn't know I was on the phone and we talked so long I fell asleep on him!"

I was destined to wind up in the back seat of Jackson's car. I had yearned to be noticed by him since I had entered the school as a freshman . . . way too young then to be attractive to a junior. But as a sophomore, with my own standout style, things had changed. We were dating—holding hands, making excuses to get released from our classes at the same time under the guise of needing to go to the bathroom. Then we'd hook up for a quick kiss and frontal grind in the balcony of the empty student auditorium.

That night in his car, we both were prepared to go further. His magician hands were magically sending my turquoise bikini cuts to my knees. While we were kissing, he began to move oddly and grope for something other than me. When I heard a crackle and felt our lips disengage, I opened my eyes as his pearly teeth bit down on a foil package and with one tug ripped it open: a condom.

A condom. Of course, we needed a condom. How responsible of him. We had talked about having sex but had not talked about the particulars. Suddenly, in the reality of the moment, everything stopped. For the first time in more than a year of being obsessed about being Jackson's girlfriend, something inside me went very quiet.

In my mind, underneath the incessant obsession with Jackson were pictures and questions I had not seen or considered.

We were about to cross an important line. Inwardly, I assessed the situation. Jackson felt me disengage and asked, "What's wrong?" I didn't answer. I didn't *know* what was wrong. But something was indeed bothering me. "Come on," he said. I looked at him, and to my surprise I said, "I can't." His brow furrowed. He did not expect this. *I* did not expect this! Again, he asked, "What's wrong?" Shaking my head, becoming more and more disengaged, I replied: "There's nothing wrong. I like you. I just can't. I'm not ready. I'm sorry."

I wasn't expecting his next question, "What are you afraid of?" but a part of me was ready with an answer. From deep within, a volcano of worry erupted: "I'm afraid maybe I don't love you, maybe I just like you a whole bunch . . . that this car is not where I want to make love for the first time . . . what if that condom breaks . . . I certainly wouldn't be happy with the consequences . . . I'm so happy you have the condom . . . I appreciate it . . . but it also reminds me that I don't know you . . . I'm too young to get pregnant . . . I'm afraid of ruining my life!" All this worry flowed like hot lava into the car, making us both uncomfortable.

My "I can't" wasn't a "real" I can't—that is, of course I could have sex. My aroused body was proof that I was physically able. But I was afraid. "I can't" in that moment wasn't about ability; it was about choices. It was suddenly about what I was choosing for my life, and what I wanted. I did not want to get pregnant, and even the slightest risk created a definite "no" to sex.

Jackson listened. He too was becoming less engaged, but he had not yet written off receiving the fruits he expected after five months of heavy petting. He leaned in to me and whispered: "You don't have to be afraid. I'm not going to get you pregnant. I can pull out at the end if you want me to, and that way you'll be safe for sure." I looked in his eyes. I liked him. But as I looked into his eyes, I couldn't see us together in the future.

I searched my mind for any evidence of him in my life. But he was not there. When I looked beyond him into my future, I was surrounded by books, with no Jackson. I looked for our children in my mind's eye. They were not there. Jackson was not in my future, yet here I was in the back seat of his car about to share one of life's best memories with him.

I am not a tease. I don't know why I hadn't taken a few moments for this sober look at my life before getting Jackson, and myself, all worked up. But there I was. The only thing I could think to say was, "I can't. I'm sorry." Hurt, he bit back, "You can, you just don't want to."

Wow. He was right. Inside of me things became quieter and clearer. My "I can't" was not the truth. The truth was I thought I wanted to, but now I didn't want to. I didn't want to continue down that path. I didn't want sex with Jackson. I liked petting. It was safe. With petting I didn't have to think about my future. But when my future and my dreams were added to the picture, no, I didn't want to have sex with Jackson.

"Come on," he tried with less commitment. And I said

again, "I can't." This "I can't" was strong without being mean. It was an "I can't" that we both knew meant "I'm not going to." My decision was made. (I was born under the astrological sign of Taurus, and they say people born under Taurus are stubborn. Without an effective argument that shifts my thinking, when I come to a decision, it is usually for good.) That last "I can't"— the one that meant "I'm not going to"—meant that it was time for us to readjust our clothes and find a way to gracefully get out of the car and say goodbye.

The lesson I learned at the expense of Jackson's sexual frustration: *I can't* is a lie. The truth is "I don't want to," "I'm not going to," "I can't imagine that I can."

On my road to inner fitness, this "I can't" lesson has helped me find my way to deeper truths for more than three decades. It has helped me guide clients to their deeper truths. When we don't explore "I can't," we live on the surface of life without acknowledging, examining, and understanding our deeper feelings. This surface surfing overlooks the truth, and as the old saying goes, the truth sets us free.

* * *

When my client Jen was offered a promotion, her first response was, "I can't." This promotion was an acknowledgment of her leadership and the faith her bosses had in her ability to perform. Jen had worked fifty- and sixty-hour weeks. She had been a listening ear and surprising leader when, during a low point in company morale, she maintained an optimistic

"We can get through this" attitude and delivered better-than-expected results. She deserved the promotion.

But Jen explained she didn't do what she did because she was trying to get promoted. The idea of the promotion made Jen despondent to the point of mild depression. She told me, "I can't accept the promotion." *(Thank God she said this to me and not her boss.)* Of course, I knew there was more to her "I can't." So, just like I did in the back seat of Jackson's car, I walked with her through her "I can't" statements to help her see the truth, as I had learned to do years earlier.

I started with a reality check. I asked whether she was physically or mentally impaired in a way that would make her unable to perform the tasks that went with the new job. She chuckled and said, "No," and then soberly, "I just can't take the job."

I explained to Jen that "I can't" would be accurate if we were talking about turning off a stove and she discovered that the knob was broken, or if she was in Hawaii and suddenly remembered that she had left the stove on in Los Angeles. Then "I can't" makes sense. I reiterated that *can't* implies physical inability. I asked, "What does 'I can't' mean to you regarding this promotion?"

She just stared at me. I was sitting with Jen but seeing myself in the car with Jackson. I pressed and asked whether "I can't" meant she didn't want to—*like it had for me*. She shook her head no.

"So, you would like the promotion?" I asked.

"Yes," she said. "But I can't take it."

I have to admit my next question was tinged with exasperation: "What does that mean?" Her answer had even more exasperation in it than my question: "It means I'm afraid! I can't imagine that I can do a good job!"

Eureka! There it was—her truth . . . not THE truth, but the truth of the limited way Jen saw herself. She saw herself as not capable. I knew that Jen had learned this from her mother, who had never applauded Jen's outstanding accomplishments or congratulated her. Instead, Jen's mother would say, "If your teachers really knew you, they would see you as a fraud." So Jen came to see herself as a fraud, and as unworthy.

This was the distorted image Jen carried about herself. The truth we would discover, however, was much more exciting. But to get there, we first had to put her history and Self-doubt on the table—uncovered and naked for us both to see.

I was excited because I knew that Jen's limited view of her Self was a habit handed to her by her mother, and it was fear—false evidence appearing real. I was confident that together we could navigate to the other side of her fear.

"I can't" rarely means that we in fact are unable to do something. It is more often an emotional bypass—a way of getting around our feelings without having to actually feel them. "I can't" is an easy way to place distance between us and our more vulnerable feelings and difficult choices. It is easier and more comfortable to say "I can't" than "I'm afraid," "I don't want to," "I don't want to do what's required," "I don't want the responsibility of this choice," "This crosses my boundary,"

"I don't know how"—or as in Jen's case, "I'm afraid that I'm not capable."

Whenever we are stuck, a deeper truth is underneath our stopping point that needs to get out. When we take a moment to listen to our Self at a deeper level, we discover deeper truths. When we become aware of our deeper truths, we can consciously choose actions that either support them or override them.

Conscious choices are better choices, because we are aware we are choosing. Choice means we've opted to take one path over another. When we know we're choosing, we can always decide to choose again. We can make a change. We can rethink, redirect, and rechoose. The ability and right to choose again and again belong to all of us, in every situation. Of course, making a new choice can be challenging. But we *can* do it.

I am sorry that Jackson probably remembers me as a tease; however, I am thrilled that I made a conscious choice about what I did not want for my life in the back seat of his car. Four years later, with the college freshman who became my first long-term relationship, I had sex for the first time. That night left me with a beautiful memory. It was full of love, openness, and mutual agreement.

Jen took the promotion, and then she earned yet another. She left her vague and scary "I can't" in my office, much the way I had left mine in Jackson's car. You can leave the lie of "I can't" behind by getting clear about what your "I can't" really means.

Inner Fitness Practice

The Big Lie

"I can't."

The Truth

"I can't" is not a choice. It is a fussy avoidance of a deeper truth.

The Possibility

Inviting clarity by acknowledging where you are and your right to consciously choose the direction that is best for you.

Try This

Make a pact with your Self to listen for your "I can't" statements. When you hear them, complete this sentence: *If I tell myself the truth, this "I can't" really means* _____ (fill in the blank).

Unresolved lies come camouflaged in many tricky, sophisticated ways.

When Was the Last Time You Said, "I'm Upset Because"?

*The tears fall, they're so easy to wipe off
onto my sleeve, but how do I erase
the stain from my heart?*

MY FATHER WAS A GREAT FATHER AND A HORRIBLE husband. As a father, he regularly played with me and my three siblings. He trusted us and told us we could do and become anything we put our minds to. He was a fair disciplinarian *(to us girls, I should say)*. And with Daddy I always felt safe. As a husband, though he loved my mother, he was terribly controlling and sometimes emotionally and physically abusive. This incongruence didn't make sense . . . until just before he died.

I remember being ten or eleven, riding in the back seat of the family car with a knot in my stomach, listening to my parents argue. Their loud voices made me and my brother and two sisters quiet and anxious. When he got mad, Daddy sometimes hit Mommy. The argument they were having felt like it could turn into a smack in any moment. And it did, right as we passed the intersection of Dempster and McCormick. In a rage, Daddy threw the car into "Park" in the middle of the street, jumped out, and went around to Mommy's side of the car. We acted fast and locked the doors. We had to.

The look in Daddy's eyes was nothing I had seen before. Mommy got into the driver's seat and aimed the car toward home. Driving slowly, she did her best to comfort us and get us all to calm down. Daddy walked home. That walk must have been good for him because it was years—maybe even a decade or more—before we kids ever saw that kind of anger surface again. It was as if Daddy had made a pact with himself to never allow himself to go ballistic and hit Mommy again. It worked . . . for a while.

Even though Daddy had locked up his anger, I came to know that the threat of it was always hanging over Mommy's head. While we kids played carefree in the park, or ran around the grocery store looking at toys, Mommy's eyes were always on the clock, knowing that she needed to complete her shopping and other errands in a reasonable amount of time. Otherwise, when she returned home, Daddy would angrily drill her about where she had been and ask suspiciously why picking up groceries took so long.

Daddy was jealous . . . insanely so. The insanely jealous part of him was not the part that loved my mother deeply. It was as if the angry person he could become was one of those body snatchers in a science fiction movie.

Years after Daddy's walk home, when I was an adult living in my own apartment, my baby sister, Pam, called. She was crying. Daddy had hit Mommy and given her a black eye. Pam is almost ten years younger, so she was unaccustomed to this side of our father. She was too young to remember Daddy's bottled rage and had seen him blow up only once: when an out-of-line neighbor stood pointing his finger in our older sister Marty's face, cursing and yelling at her. Marty was fourteen or fifteen years old at the time, measuring five-feet-two-inches tall. The man was six-foot-three-inches. Daddy had warned the neighbor twice before to stay off our property. This time, when the man's loud voice pulled Daddy from the backyard to the front, and Daddy saw this 6'3" figure standing over Marty yelling, he saw red. He became a bull. We remember that blowup as evidence of Daddy's love and protection, not his rage. Even today when I think about Daddy, I think about the power of both his love and his fight.

As Daddy aged, his anger increased, and he became outright abusive to our mother. Whatever pact he had made all those years before, he broke. Even his tone toward me became more aggressive. I wondered why he was so angry. The answer came from a court-ordered counseling session after he had choked my mother and she filed a complaint and divorce papers, after forty-four years of marriage.

In that counseling session Daddy told the counselor a story he had never shared with another human being: When he was eight or nine years old, he came home early from school and saw his mother having sex with a family friend.

After that counseling session, in a moment more vulnerable than any I've ever seen, my father sat on my couch and shared with me this story that had tortured him his entire life. He revealed that the picture of his mother with that man replayed in his mind every day. It was his sacred torture—that secret which haunts us and often winds up controlling our lives in some way. And no matter how it tortures us, we feel married to it—for better or for worse. Daddy's sacred torture was the reason he was angry. Old hurt, inflamed and tender, was locked and swollen inside of him.

Years later, when I attended a two-year course in Spiritual Psychology, I learned of the concept of *I'm upset because* . . . The professors, Ron and Mary Hulnick, explained that *I'm upset because* is a misconception in that we believe whatever follows the *because* is responsible for our being upset. "I'm upset because you won't listen" means that I believe *you* are making me upset. We make something outside of us the reason for our upset. When we think that other people and things cause us to be upset, we can never get to the core of the upset.

The truth is, our upset already lives inside of us. A previous unresolved emotional experience placed it there. In the case of my parents' relationship, Daddy operated as though my mother's behavior was the reason for his being upset. He would say, *I'm upset because it shouldn't take two hours to shop for groceries. I'm upset because you were leaning in and smiling while you were talking to that guy.* The truth is that Daddy was upset because his mother had violated her marriage vows and betrayed his father, and he had witnessed it. He was upset because he had never found the words to say, *This happened to me and it still hurts.*

The Hulnicks explained that our real upset is always deeper than the "because" we assign to it. In other words, there is no such thing as *I'm upset because.* The more accurate sentence is simply *I'm upset.* Upset already lives within me, and this experience triggers it.

Daddy was carrying torturous anger and upset. This is why he blew up easily and needed to control things. Witnessing his mother's betrayal of his beloved father left Daddy feeling personally betrayed. This hurt became the stabbing upset that bled into his life. It destroyed his marriage.

Unresolved upset is like an open wound. It is full of pus and tender with hurt until we give our Self the attention that allows the healing process to begin.

The pact Daddy made with himself on his walk home that night is a testament to his willpower. But will is never a cure. On that walk, I guess Daddy decided to exercise his will over the upset inside of him. He told himself he would not behave that way ever again. His willpower allowed us kids years of treasured family memories. I truly believe this was Daddy's goal. To this day, I feel he was one of the best daddies a girl could ask for. But in the end, Daddy's walk did not heal and vanquish the upset inside of him. Instead, it sent it to a deeper hiding place where it could fester and become even more tender and painful.

Saying *This happened to me and it still hurts* is the starting point of our healing.

When we don't address our pain, we begin to feel that it's bigger and stronger than we are. Because my father never risked talking about his sacred torture, he could not activate the healing process. He could not learn to forgive his mother, nor could he let go of his anger. This created for him torturous isolation.

Healing starts with an acknowledgment of what happened and how it made us feel. Then come understanding, forgiveness, and more productive and empowering perspectives. Daddy's sacred torture left him with a belief that drove a nail into the heart of his marriage: *I can't trust even the best woman in the world.*

I'm upset because statements are lies that obscure the real source of our hurt and discomfort. The truth: *When we feel intense anger, rage, or seemingly irrational upset, unresolved feelings from the past are fueling our reactions.* When it comes to dissolving pain, we must start by looking within.

The act of looking within is not a passive one. It's courageous and dynamic. You can begin to look within by asking yourself this question the next time you find yourself upset, triggered, or behaving irrationally: *When was the first time I felt this way or experienced this kind of reaction?* This question can take us to a stored memory that holds answers.

Whatever your answer, sit in your observer's chair (see Question 2) and look at the old memory. Put it on a split screen—the old memory on one side, and the current triggered event on the other—and then observe similar feelings, beliefs, and assumptions. You may be surprised to find that your current reaction is connected to an old event that lives in your stored memory.

* * *

Looking within is a profound act of Self-care. It sends the message *I matter* to every cell in our bodies. All living things, including our own cells, respond to such care. A dog wags its tail and plants grow when we give them time and attention. Our inner wholeness also blossoms when we show ourselves Self-care. Looking within is the critical first step. It empowers us to stand up to festering unresolved upset, take control of it, and allow it to unravel and heal.

I have had clients and students doubt that "looking within" is enough. They say, "But what should I *do*?" The answer: *Looking within is a huge action. It opens all other doors.* It will naturally lead you to other acts of Self-care that foster healing.

The one thing I stress with my clients is that they first adopt the "inward glance attitude" before they look within. The inward glance attitude says, *No matter what I see, I will not judge myself. I will not hold a grudge. I will deeply and profoundly love and accept myself and give myself permission to let go, forgive, and move on. I will be grateful for the awareness, and grateful that I can live my life more fully from this point forward.*

An inward glance will soak into the hard ground underneath the upset and reveal the assumptions we've made and the conclusions we've drawn about our Self and life.

Daddy's upset was connected to his conclusion that good women and wives cheat. Had he learned to look within, he could have cultivated the ability to separate his feelings for his wife from his feelings for his mother; he would have been able to catch himself when he began to unconsciously direct the anger and distrust toward his wife that were actually feelings he held toward his mother.

To dissolve our upset, we must take the look within that healing and freedom require. If you yearn to feel comfortable in your own skin, you must first get curious about the assumptions you've made about life, the conclusions you've drawn, and what is underneath your reactions. This kind of Self-observing forges inner fitness.

Acknowledging and appropriately addressing what's going on inside of us leads to the realization that we are more than any event, hurtful experience, or pain we encounter. No upset in our lives is bigger than we are. None—no matter how old or challenging it may feel. Daring to take action and make choices as though this concept is true empowers us with the inner strength to risk looking at scary, painful memories.

Daddy's life and marriage would have been better had he forced himself—for the purpose of healing—to share with his wife his hurtful childhood memory. Sharing our hurt with someone with whom we feel safe, seen, and heard takes the sting out of our pain. It emboldens us to say and feel more.

It is possible to take our power back from old memories and hurts, to let go of *I'm upset because* statements and release all people and things from the responsibility of making us happy. Begin by telling yourself, *I'm acknowledging my hurt and letting go of the false assumptions and hurtful conclusions I've drawn. I'm letting in the light of forgiveness. I'm ready to heal.*

Inner Fitness Practice

The Big Lie

Other people and things cause you to be upset.

The Truth

Your upset already lives within you. The current "upsetting" experience has triggered the pain of your unresolved emotions. If you think that *I'm upset because* is the answer, recognize that what follows the word *because* is not the truth. It's a justification.

The Possibility

Acknowledging old unaddressed hurt and thereby leaving that hurt behind. Instead of *I'm upset because* statements, your future can be full of statements like *I'm happy because . . . I'm excited because . . . I'm okay because . . .*

Try This

What feeling statement do you frequently make? Fill in the blank with that feeling.

I'm _____ because _____.

1. Take a day or week and listen to these statements. Write them down when you think them or hear them come out of your mouth: *I'm disappointed because you did that. I'm irritated because of the traffic.*

2. Get curious about the statements you use most often. Lovingly ask yourself, *Why do I feel (upset, irritated, depressed, scared) so often? When did this habit start?*

3. Whatever you find, don't judge it. No matter how the habit began, use this acceptance statement: Lovingly say to yourself, *I deeply and profoundly love and accept myself and give myself permission to let go of the past and move on.*

4. Whenever these statements or other discoveries come up, repeat this Self-acceptance statement.

When we brush by painful experiences and neglect our Self-care, we lose our connection to Self.

What If "One Day" Starts TODAY?

The future starts today, not tomorrow.
—POPE JOHN PAUL II

REMEMBER WHEN YOU COULDN'T WAIT TO BE SIX YEARS old? Six is the age every four- or five-year-old dreams of reaching. Six was the age I thought I'd become a big girl. Toothless and excited, I waited for my sixth birthday like it was Christmas. I don't know now exactly what made six so important. I do know that soon after turning six, I was waiting for the day I would turn ten, then sixteen. Restless still, I put my sights on eighteen, then blew past it headed to twenty-one, twenty-five . . . and thirty. Whatever I was expecting from each of these magical markers kept eluding me, leaving me a bit undersatisfied and therefore rushing ahead to the next marker in hopes of one day reaching my happily-ever-after life—the "one day" that would magically transform my life never came.

"One day"—when life is better—is a lie that can take half a lifetime to see. **"One day" brings us nothing if we don't learn what "today" has to teach us.** I refer to *one-day thinking* as chasing the future at the expense of today. It's a ruthless, irrational no-win game, because it mows past the present moment looking for something better, as though the present moment doesn't count.

The present gets treated like that great girlfriend or boyfriend who is overlooked in the pursuit of greener pastures. The tragedy is that the more we focus on "one day," the less we see today. And, of course, today is the only road we can take to "one day."

My client Joseph, a brilliant systems engineer in the computer world, had his "one day" all planned out. His problem was that he kept jumping over today in his rush to "one day." He told himself that one day he would be the boss of his world; one day he would have enough money to never be affected by another person's whims; one day he would meet the woman he could fall in love with; one day he would be happy.

Joseph thought he was prepared for his one day when he would have career success. Everyone saw him as super smart. He was a disciplined thinker, he was competitive, and he had graduated from a good school. These attributes advanced his career. He became a department head and leader of thirty-two people.

There was just one problem. Joseph was not *prepared* to be a leader of people. He had dreamed of one day being acknowledged for technological breakthroughs, not for being the leader of people. Actually, he didn't like people. "People are basically unreliable, incompetent assholes," he told me during our first session. *(I had been recommended to him after a leadership assessment revealed that Joseph's people skills needed support.)*

It didn't take long for us to get to stories of Joseph's parents leaving him to prepare his own meals and to walk two miles alone to school at age six. Joseph told me that when he was seven, his father promised to pick him up from school, but after that morning's promise, Joseph never saw his father again. He waited at school for two hours before he made the two-mile walk back home. Then, he and his mother and sister waited for days for that difficult, brooding man to return. But he never did.

Long before he said it, I knew Joseph had not emotionally acknowledged the loss of his father. His tightly set jaw and stories that painted him as easily irritated and inflexible were my indicators.

When I asked Joseph questions about his father, his responses were cool and dispassionate. He refused to think that his father affected him or his success. Without the slightest hint of caring, Joseph said, "He doesn't mean anything to me. He doesn't factor into the equation."

These statements would later be revealed as lies. Not the kind of lie we tell when we are trying to persuade someone of something we know is not true, but the kind of lie we tell to ourselves when what is true is too much to bear.

These lies get packaged as rage, isolation, drug addiction, and other destructive behaviors. This was the kind of lie that Joseph told when he said about his father, "He doesn't mean anything to me." Joseph couldn't see that his focus on *"one day* when he was successful" had helped him to ignore the pain and disappointment he felt *today*. He didn't realize that the emotions he overlooked today would affect his success "one day."

Our hurts, dramas, traumas, upsets, disappointments, and fears don't politely dissolve and make room for our "one day" to arrive. They travel with us. When we accomplish the "one day" we've worked to create, our unaddressed feelings are right there, waiting. Usually, their presence confuses us and causes anger and resentment. It's easy to become resentful when we think that "one day" we will have enough—power, money, time, friends, love, sex—and then discover that these *things* don't change how we feel inside.

* * *

When it comes to life, rushing to *one day when life is better* is like stepping over the basics of arithmetic and algebra headed for calculus. Joseph stepped over a number of opportunities to address smoldering feelings. He neglected to take advantage of the information his "todays" and "yesterdays" were giving him.

There was a time when a new girlfriend promised to do something with him and then canceled at the last minute. Joseph was so angry he punched and shattered the bathroom mirror. There was also the time he blew up at a New York taxi driver for choosing the couple standing next to him. He didn't recognize that his uncommonly harsh reactions were indicators of an old wound that was asking to be acknowledged so it could heal.

Had Joseph stopped to question his "today," explore his feelings, acknowledge both his dreams and his disappointments, his unresolved feelings would have revealed themselves. They would have guided him through the hurt he was running from.

Pain goes away only when we acknowledge it. The truth is that we must learn to sit down with the past instead of run from it, speak the unspoken to our Self, and breathe. As we breathe and learn to take an objective (observer's chair) look at the past, we discover assumptions we've made about our Self, conclusions we've drawn against our Self, and subtle ways we consistently reject our Self. We can then open our lives to new, more rewarding possibilities. As Joseph began to take care of his Self by looking within, he saw the lies—misconceptions— he harbored about both his Self and his father.

Through developing an inner fitness mindset and practice, Joseph gained a more objective and compassionate view of himself. He realized that he had interpreted his father's dramatic exit from his life to mean that he, Joseph, was repulsive and unworthy. This unconscious idea of his Self left Joseph feeling isolated and angry. He developed the protective reflex of rejecting people first before they could reject him like he perceived his father had done.

By engaging in internal practices that helped him to center and redefine himself and calm his explosive reactions, Joseph was able to revisit moments and feelings he had rushed past. He began to remember subtleties about life with his father: the way his father spent hours in the garage alone, and how, when Joseph would ask him the kinds of questions a bright, budding computer mind might ask, his father often dropped his head, unable to answer. Joseph's heart softened as he saw for the first time his father's low Self-esteem. Joseph began to suspect that his father's choice to leave him and the family was not a statement about who he, Joseph, was but a statement about his father's feelings of personal inadequacy.

Because Joseph was no longer running from the past or closed off from it, he could see the past more clearly. Acknowledging our feelings makes room for new realizations. As Joseph looked back on his life with a desire to understand versus judge, he was surprised to discover that he and his father were not that different. Neither knew how to express his feelings. Both chose to distance themselves from people as their way of managing life. At one point, Joseph looked at me with a softness that had been waiting in the wings of his life and said, "I think my father did the best he could. He didn't know any better. I don't think he knew he mattered."

Big events happen to all of us. They matter. **Avoiding big**

events by rushing past them to *one day when life is better* is a plan for disaster. Avoiding dangers such as hot stoves, cliff edges, and toxic people is smart. Avoiding issues that are present in our lives, such as traumatic events and recurring fear and anger, or avoiding issues related to how we see our Self is not a sound strategy. Every time we avoid our feelings today, we set ourselves up for inevitable sadness "one day."

To get to "one day," we must invest in today.

Today is where the choices live that create tomorrow. Today may come with challenges, but those challenges also house opportunities. Inner fitness practices such as viewing our lives from our director's chair, acknowledging our feelings, interrupting our habitual way of thinking about the past, and daring to contemplate new possibilities will reveal hidden opportunities. These thriving Self choices prepare us for the good that is headed in our direction. When we rush past today, we squander any chance for a truly fulfilling *one day when life is better.*

The truth is, there is no moment or "one day" when life stops being life. To meet life, we must be present today, take that inward glance which connects us to the truth, and acknowledge what we feel so we can one day stand in front of our dream come true and be able to embrace it.

Inner Fitness Practice

The Big Lie

One day, when life gets better, you'll be happy.

The Truth

When you unconsciously hold on to hurt, it shows up in other areas of your life. You can't reach your full potential until you give your unresolved feelings the loving attention they require in order to heal.

The Possibility

Learning to acknowledge and be with difficult feelings, and forge the strength and ability to meet and navigate life no matter what comes.

Try This

1. Step outside of yourself and observe your behavior. If you are reacting; arguing a lot; feeling unseen, unheard, or unsafe, find the "yesterday" moment that you rushed past.

2. Find a loving way to engage with yourself right where you are. Feel your feelings. Write in a journal, rock yourself like a baby, pretend to be the

best loving parent you can imagine to that hurt part of you. Open your heart to whatever degree you can in that moment.

3. Tell yourself: *I matter. I am worthy. I have value.* Do this whenever you feel your heart closing or you feel yourself rushing past a moment because you don't want to feel.

Today allows us to acquire the tools and gain the perspective needed to build our most fulfilling and fully alive life.

QUESTION 9

What Is Real Confidence?

I am bigger than this feeling or experience.
It does not define me, and it is not here to
pull me under. It is here to lift me up!

IN JUNIOR HIGH SCHOOL, WHERE RELATIONSHIPS HAVE THE life span of a fly, for two months I had a best friend named Valarie. She was what the old folks call a hot mess—meaning she was not everything she appeared to be. Valarie was a cute, petite girl with slightly bowed legs, a curvy body, a big fluffy afro to die for, and lips that Angelina Jolie would covet. Her voice was naturally sexy—like her whole life she was recovering from a cold. Her laugh was unique and infectious. It is no surprise that all the boys at Pasteur Junior High were in love with her . . . all of them.

Valarie walked the halls turning heads and giving off a scent that left guys panting. Most assumed she was way out of their league, so they never followed her scent to get an up-close smell. Had they—like I eventually did—they would have followed her right out of class, down the hall, and through the back gate where she regularly sat with a bunch of guys and a girl or two "downing" yellow jackets and red devil pills, smoking weed, and eventually shooting heroin. That's the hot mess part.

When old folks refer to someone as a hot mess, it's a warning, one I heard a thousand times growing up, said in a thousand different ways: "Don't judge a book by its cover." "Everything that glitters ain't gold." "Pretty is as pretty does." "Just 'cause something looks a certain way doesn't mean it's so." All these sayings applied to Valarie. They are the reason our friendship ended quickly. What I didn't know is how they also applied to me, and how Valarie would teach me the true meaning of confidence: *Confidence is the ability to face the more complicated, messy, and often scary stuff inside of us.*

I was envious that Valarie could part a sea of admiring boys as she confidently walked down a hallway. Confident people are definitely the superstars in school, and in our society. They are our gladiators—you know, those fighters back in ancient Rome who fought an opponent to the death or in other ways wrestled life to the ground in front of cheering fans. Valarie's hip-swinging strut—head held high—was her gladiator stride.

In boardrooms, walking across stages, in front of cameras, or on schoolyards, today's gladiators lead with the sword of confidence. They fight to the death, winning arguments, fans, sales contracts, elections, Super Bowls, and lovers.

We all play the role of the gladiator at some point. I love those days when the gladiator in me rises. On more than a few occasions I've stood at a closed door, taken a deep breath, and told myself to enter a room like I own it. Be Serena Williams or Michael Jordan in the zone. Then, with a gladiator's stride and steel spine, I've opened that door prepared to win and crossed the threshold with my "game-on" face to meet the questions or experiences that waited.

* * *

However, no matter how confident our strut, every person has a troubling area where fear and insecurity show up. This is the stuff of life most people don't talk about. I didn't. Acknowledging fear in a society that does not talk about fear can lose contracts, jobs, and respect.

There was a time when if I witnessed someone's insecurity, a part of me would back away from them, keeping my distance for fear I might catch what they have. As I backed away, under my breath I'd give thanks that I wasn't that person and didn't have that problem. This was during my ignorant years when I thought I knew more about life than I did.

Back then, when my good friend and novelist Bebe Moore Campbell was alive, I remember a part of me "backing away" from her as she disclosed to me and a small group of friends her fear of flying and riding in elevators. I was stunned as her already fair skin went white when she talked about her fears and how they complicated her life. Her fears made no sense to me. They seemed unnecessary, irrational. As I had flippantly done with Valarie in junior high school, I concluded that Bebe's poise and tigerlike ability to take charge of life was a pretense, a lie.

As Bebe spoke, I thought, "Wow, she is a hot mess!"—that is, full of insecurities that no one would ever imagine. I literally said to myself, *Boy I'm glad that is not me.* If you are thinking, *Wow, Tina, how insensitive and arrogant,* you are right. My "I'm above that" response to Bebe's naked sharing is the very reason people lead with confidence and don't admit to insecurity. None of us want people to write us off, to think less of us, or to see us as a hot mess. But like my daddy used to say, "Eventually, arrogance will humble you."

Here's how time has humbled me. When Bebe spoke of her fear of riding in elevators and flying in planes, my own unspoken fears and challenges *never* crossed my mind. Because my periodic fear of auditioning didn't look like Bebe's fear of elevators, I didn't see the similarities. Arrogance jumped ahead of empathy.

Years later, when my old auditioning fear was triggered, I saw that underneath the "look" of things, Bebe and I were the same. We were both periodically burdened by a fear that seemed to have a mind all its own. To say I was humbled by this realization is an understatement. Indeed, there are times when the folly of pride is so great that every person we've ever judged crosses our minds, and in our hearts we apologize and with a whispered voice ask the heavens for forgiveness.

When a bout with my auditioning fear stormed into my life, it was so uncomfortable that my whole sense of self was affected. How could I feel a gladiator's confidence in so many ways and in this area feel at risk and out of control? Was I a fraud?

The lie in all this is the idea that a whole person can be defined by either confidence or insecurity, not both. Insecure moments do not make our areas of confidence a lie. Valarie's strut was real, and so was her pain. Bebe was brilliant and fierce in many real and powerful ways, but she had not yet figured out how to use her power to support herself in her areas of greatest challenge.

Confidence doesn't mean we've got it all together, nor does insecurity mean we're a hot mess or a fraud.

* * *

For years, the incongruence of being authentically confident in many areas and insecure in others vexed me. I would sometimes literally ask out loud to the ever-listening universe, *How can this be? (Remember that I said that often when I am trying to figure something out I go to sleep and dream the answer.)* It was my dream of meeting the three parts of me on the beach—my surviving self, my thriving Self, and the infinite SELF—that elegantly resolved this question for me: In my areas of insecurity, my reactive surviving self held the reins. In my areas of confidence, I led with the traits of a higher Self. Seeing this clearly set me on the course of working with my areas of insecurity and challenge from a whole new mindset. My thriving Self and infinite SELF became my teachers.

* * *

Behind every lie lives an awakening that makes the lie worth the pain and effort it has caused. My revelation was that no one is all confidence or all insecurity.

I had to learn that when a part of me struggles with insecurity, it means the insecure part is simply asking for help. Insecurity needs the confident part of us to "be with it" without judgment. This means being a good friend to the insecure part, giving this part the support and guidance it needs to help it find its way—instead of hating it, disowning it, and turning our backs to it.

I loved my confidence and disliked my insecurity. I saw insecurity as weak and unacceptable. This is like loving life but rejecting death. It's irrational. The two are partners. To know one, we must be aware of the other. To always be confident and never be insecure is not human. I began to see that confidence and insecurity work together in strengthening our lives.

Confidence is not "better," it's stronger. It is connected to an inner sense of ourselves that accepts life as a journey and trusts that our inner Self is there to lovingly and capably guide us.

Confidence points to the areas in our lives where we "show up" fully. It reveals the beliefs we carry that make us strong. Examine your areas of confidence and you will find thriving Self characteristics: a strong sense of your Self and innate worth and capableness, and an air of enthusiasm and aliveness. Insecurity is filled with doubt. Doubt is a surviving self attribute because it points to the areas where we don't know our Self or don't trust our inner Self to show up. Insecurity reveals the beliefs that must be traded in or reconstructed in order to make ourselves strong.

When we judge or reject the insecure part of ourselves, we are like a parent judging or rejecting a child—instead of unconditionally loving that child, knowing that child is capable, and helping that child find his or her way.

When I told myself the truth about those times I backed away from people, I realized those were actually *my* moments of insecurity. I needed to create distance between myself and the disquieting fears and behaviors of others because *I* was afraid. I feared their vulnerability, because I feared that my own vulnerability—unleashed—could topple me and pull me under. Unconsciously, I kept safe emotional distance from other people's pain in an effort to distance myself from my own uncertainties. I trampled over uncomfortable feelings, ignored them, or backed away from them.

This is how my perceived confidence was a lie in my life.

When we use confidence to compensate for unacknowledged insecurity, hurt, fear, or other uncomfortable emotions, it is a lie that our small fearful self tells us in a desperate effort to feel safe and in control.

Through The Inner Fitness Project, I began to see and work with insecurity in new ways. I now acknowledge insecurity without focusing on it or judging it. For example: If I notice that my heart feels tight, instead of running from this feeling or ignoring it, I lovingly and warmly touch my heart area and breathe deeply. I imagine the warmth of my hand and loving Self-acceptance melting the discomfort. I acknowledge my discomfort yet focus on the other parts of me that are not engaged in the fear or discomfort. This reminds me that there is more to me than this feeling of discomfort.

It is fascinating to feel my heart pumping with fear, place my hand on my heart, focus on the quiet stillness in maybe my legs or buttocks, and experience the discomfort recede to the background as the awareness of the calm, centered, and strong parts come to the foreground. I usually affirm in these moments that I am more than this discomfort and that there is nothing on the other side of God. *(A great example of the power of specifically acknowledging a problem without judging it, or ourselves, is part of the brilliance of the EFT process mentioned in Question 4. The first step in applying EFT is to design an affirmation that acknowledges the problem and at the same time affirms Self-love. It might look something like this:* Even though I feel insecure and anxious, I deeply and profoundly love and accept myself.)

Honestly acknowledging a problem or emotional difficulty that we face supports the mind and heart in healing.

***

I began to make peace with insecurity. I realized that insecurity doesn't mean "weak," "not good enough," or "fraud." Over and over, when I was in the midst of any old uncomfortable feelings, I would tell myself, *I am bigger than this feeling or experience. It does not define me, and it is not here to pull me under. It is here to lift me up!*

I realized that true confidence required just one thing of me: *to be with what was uncomfortable without judging myself.* I needed to trust that there is an innately whole part of me that is confidently—albeit mystically—poised to show me the way to turn discomfort and insecurity into personal power, Self-acceptance, and peace.

Today, I trust that my inner Self can show me how to transform discomfort into power. As my default starting point, I expect an eventual and inevitable positive outcome. This attitude and effort mystically bring new information and people into my life. They come as messengers, teachers, or resources that point me in the direction of the answers I seek.

Through Self-acceptance I began to adopt a healthy "so what" attitude that looks like this: *So what if I get nervous and feel insecure before or during auditions? I am more than this old pattern. Even in the midst of this challenge, I can achieve success and live a powerful and satisfying life. Plus, I can turn to stress-reduction exercises to help me with this.*

This "so what" attitude rewired my experience with insecurity. Instead of adding the stress of judgment and Self-attack to my disquiet, it stopped my harsh Self-judgment cold and stimulated Self-intimacy, hope, and greater inner freedom.

We no longer need to resist, judge, or blame any aspect of ourselves when insecurity shows up, nor regret any aspect of our life's journey. When we accept our Self, we are free to see insecurity and all emotions as passing feelings, instead of fixed, permanent states. "I am feeling insecure" is an accurate statement. It represents a changing moment in time. "I am insecure" is not accurate, however. It is a false statement—a lie—because we are more than our passing feelings, just like we are more than the annoying or disappointing summer cold we might be forced to manage. Like the cold, emotional experiences will pass—if we let them. We do that by not hanging on to them, beating ourselves up because of them, or using them to define us in any way.

Nowadays, when fear or insecurity is triggered inside of me, I have learned to quell those feelings by saying over and over to myself, *I am MORE than this.* When you recognize that you are so much more than this or that, you can more comfortably and more confidently "be with" what shows up.

* * *

I often think about my two-month BFF Valarie. I play a game inside my heart. I see her walking down the hallway turning heads. She is aware of her power. She walks through the back gates, past the world of drugs she used to feel safe, and makes her way to someone who listens to her fears and pain without backing away. That person listens in a way that helps Valarie remember that she is MORE. I see her take a deep breath, cry the tears that need to be shed, let go of the past, and see herself as MORE . . . and I see the same for you.

Inner Fitness Practice

The Big Lie

Because you lack confidence in an area, that means you're basically insecure.

The Truth

Real confidence is the ability to face the more complicated, messy, and often scary stuff inside of you. Self-acceptance builds core strength. The confidence that comes with knowing you have innate value is the foundation you need for true confidence.

The Possibility

Moving beyond shame and embarrassment into Self-love and understanding, even when insecurity shows up or you feel overwhelmed.

Try This

1. When feelings of insecurity come up, acknowledge them instead of denying them.

2. Become proactive instead of reactive. Example: In the midst of insecurity, ask yourself, *What is the small idea of myself that I have come to believe?*

3. Tell yourself, *I am MORE than this small idea.* From this point forward, *this idea or challenge can change.*

4. Affirm: *I deeply and profoundly love and accept myself in this moment, and I allow myself to grow and change.*

5. Be patient with yourself and life. Readjust in this way as often as you need.

*When you know yourself,
you are empowered;
when you accept yourself,
you are invincible.*

Are You Stuck in
I Thought I Was Done
with That! Thinking?

I thought I was over you. I thought
I'd moved on. I thought you were gone.
I guess I was wrong.

A NEW CLIENT, CARRIE, SAT ON THE FLOOR, LEGS CROSSED, head down, bewildered and angry with herself. Her eyes were red. White tissue snowballs gathered at her right knee. She was shaking her head. It went back and forth in that slow way that happens when we replay a scene in our minds that we feel we should have handled differently, or a scene we believe never should have happened in the first place.

Carrie had done it again. She had fallen in love with another married man. With a dazed, unfocused stare she muttered, "How did I let this happen, again?" She had just told me that dating married men had been a pattern in her life. Like the force that inevitably pulls water spinning down a drain, Carrie over and over found herself in the emotional whirlwind that goes with getting involved with married men: First, the excitement of meeting someone special—the long, effortless conversations that quickly unwrap deep caring and ignite uncontrollable feelings. These feelings quickly turn into attachment and thoughts of a future together. Then, the torture of checking the phone and feeling confused or scared when he doesn't call. Followed by the joy and romance of his showing up at the door, unannounced, hungry for love, and then peacefully cuddling in the aftermath of passion. Finally, the painful reality as he gets up, showers, and leaves—to go home to his wife. Again. And again.

From the age of seventeen, Carrie fell in love with men who were married or seriously involved with someone else. Either way, they were not totally available. Carrie hated the helpless, stuck feeling this pattern caused her.

In her late twenties Carrie swore "No more" after watching her then "boyfriend" shower and dress, fish through his pockets for his wedding ring, put it on, kiss Carrie on her forehead, and leave. Yet in spite of her swears and promises, men with wives kept crashing into Carrie's world.

Fed up with this pain, Carrie found a therapist in whose office she experienced life-altering clarity. "In a flash, everything made sense," she told me. All the puzzle pieces of her life instantly formed a complete picture. She saw how every man she had ever loved or pined over, even her eighth-grade first love, Carlos, had been just like her father.

To the preteen Carrie, Carlos Sanchez was everything. She spent the eighth grade trying to get him to see her and want to be her boyfriend. But Carlos treated Carrie just like her father treated her—like he barely knew she was alive. Carrie's father was an emotionally unavailable man, whose heart, she said, "always felt miles away." As a child Carrie had interpreted her father's emotional unavailability to mean that he found her unworthy of his love.

Carrie's moment of clarity in the therapist's office let her see how she grasped for love. It was as if inside of her stood a little girl with her arms forever outstretched reaching up for her father, wanting him to see her, pick her up, hold her. Instead, more often than not, he didn't see her. Sometimes he even ignored her.

In her moment of clarity, Carrie saw a lifetime of behaviors for what they were. She was constantly reaching for her father's love, always trying to prove her worth. In each breakup, it was her boyfriend who left. No matter how poorly Carrie was treated, she would never leave—just like she never left her father. But with each lover who left, Carrie felt like her father was walking out on her. When she cried, her tears belonged to the little girl inside of her.

With these new insights, Carrie began to change her life.

She had learned to smell a married man a mile away and say "No thank you" to his seductive attention. But sitting on my floor three years later, she was devastated: "How did this happen? I thought I was done with that."

My heart melted for her. I knew her agony. I too had wrestled with old stuff, thought I was free of it, and then found myself blindsided by an old familiar pattern or two.

Sitting on my floor Carrie told me about the relationship that she had just broken off. She had been dating Francisco a year before she discovered that he was yet another married man, with a wife and kids in Peru. This accidental discovery was made fewer than five minutes after one of Carrie and Francisco's most "intense lovemaking sessions," when Carrie found a letter lying on Francisco's bathroom floor. As she read the letter, every cell in her body wanted to disbelieve the words, which mentioned love, children, and future plans. Carrie took the letter and dropped it on the bed where Francisco waited for her to return. She collected her clothes, and with very few words she walked out of Francisco's life.

She cried as she shared this story with me. Carrie's real pain appeared to be her inability to leave behind the pattern of falling in love with married men. She was angry with herself. She had been consciously building her inner fitness. She thought her life-changing insights in therapy and her new resolve a few years earlier had guaranteed that she would never again watch a lover shower and then go home to his wife. The blindsiding truth that Francisco was married made Carrie think she was back to square one. This was an excruciating thought; all the work she had put into changing her life didn't make a difference.

What Carrie didn't know yet was what I had learned through my own painful trials and errors, and that is, *our greatest challenges and deepest wounds must recur in order for us to heal them.* ***Thinking we are "done" with this or that issue, such that similar circumstances never again knock on our door, is a lie.***

This lie sets us up to feel like a failure when scenarios we thought we were done with happen again. Yet happen again, they will. Once a pattern is established in our lives, similar events occur over and over—to give us the opportunity to unravel our confusion and make empowering Self-care choices we did not make the first time around.

I knew that regardless of the devastation Carrie was feeling, she had made progress. I detected signs of it in her story. I felt certain that walking out of Francisco's life after she found the letter was new behavior for Carrie. She had stated that in the past, no matter how she was treated, she never left a relationship. Leaving Francisco and not looking back was a triumphant act of Self-love that Carrie was not able to see yet. She was focused on seeing herself as a failure because she thought she was "done with all that." But with the new response of walking out the door, Carrie was changing an old, well-worn pattern.

* * *

Carrie didn't know that no matter how strong our resolve, our deep emotional programming, beliefs, and patterns don't give up easily. They don't just walk away from us feeling defeated. Just like every living thing fights to live, our old patterns fight to hold on to us and have their way. Like spoiled, overly indulged children, our old pains and challenges throw tantrums and manipulate in all kinds of ways, trying to keep things as they have always been. They will even play dead and wait sometimes for years before they spring forth to grab at us and try to hold on to our lives. When these old bullies revisit us, we need our Self-love and resolve the most.

After her life-changing experience in therapy, Carrie had dated in new and healthy ways for a year and a half. Every day she seemed farther and farther removed from her old pattern of falling in love with unavailable men. So Francisco felt like a failure.

Carrie had been staring at her hands cupped in her lap as she told me her story. She desperately tried to assure herself that she had properly "vetted" Francisco. She *had* asked him the hard questions that she used to neglect: *Are you married? Do you have children? Are you in a committed relationship?* She had looked for signs of dishonesty in his words and behavior. No alarms went off. Yet Francisco had slipped through. Old familiar feelings of shame and unworthiness were beginning to surface in Carrie. She called herself a stupid fool. And, again, she lamented, "I thought I was done with that." I knew this was where the real work would begin.

I asked Carrie what hurt more—finding out that Francisco was married, or her conclusion that she was a failure? The question stunned her into silence. Finally, her answer was the same as my own answer when I learned the power of this question. Carrie's pain stemmed from judgments she had heaped on herself because of her circumstance. She would have to start with her Self-judgment in order to free herself from the recurring pattern of choosing married men.

***

Carrie's retreat to Self-judgment was as well-worn a pattern in her life as her magnetic pull to unavailable men. This was the two-step dance (actually three-step dance) that she had been dancing her whole adult life: (1) falling in love with an unavailable man, (2) watching him get up and leave, and (3) heaping on herself feelings of shame and unworthiness and lots of harsh Self-judgment.

Carrie had ended each painful breakup with even more painful Self-judgment. Her pattern of choosing unavailable men wasn't complete until it had been neatly tied together with a nasty bow of Self-rejection. What Carrie didn't know was that her Self-judgment was the icing on top of the pattern. It was proof to the tantrum-throwing pattern that it had won. Things were the same. The pattern had survived and would live on.

I was ready for Carrie. My own life had prepared me. I too had experienced frustration to the point of tears trying to leave unwanted patterns behind. My auditioning craziness, my own attraction to dysfunctional men, and the guilt that showed up as codependence regarding my brother's drug addiction had been my teachers. Whenever an old pattern recurred, I too had the sickening feeling of having to revisit painful feelings after thinking I was "done with that."

Just like Carrie, when old circumstances revisited, my heart ached as I concluded that the previous gains and heartfelt resolve I had made had slipped through my fingers in a backslide. As I found myself once again battling with a challenge that felt bigger than me, I wondered whether I would ever be free.

When the overwhelming event passed, hours, days, or weeks later, and I was out of the quicksand of the experience, I would fear, hope, and pray that it never happened again. But it did . . . again and again—in spite of my many moments of triumphant resolve. Our patterns don't change until we choose to deeply love and accept our Self even in the worst of circumstances. That was the breakthrough our session provided for Carrie. Her Self-rejection was a part of the pattern.

* * *

For our deepest wounds to heal, the kind of event or circumstances that created the wound in the first place must recur. The recurrence is our opportunity to respond differently than the way we did the first time. Healing happens when we change our old response and respond with more Self-acceptance and love.

Most people think that a recurrence is evidence that nothing has changed. In truth, however, recurring events are the opportunity we *need* for change to occur. When we experience dramatic events and lovingly hang on to a strong, healthy idea of our Self, the events do not leave a scar. **Scars are left when we add Self-rejection to dramatic events.** When we allow an event to paint us as "less than" or "not good enough" or broken in some way, we add salt to a wound. This drives the pain deeper. *Seeing our pattern through the lens of Self-love makes a powerful antidote.*

Self-love starts with an unwavering commitment to the idea that we are innately worthy. It does not matter if we doubt this in the beginning—just making space for this idea is powerful.

Carrie had interpreted her father's distance to mean she was unworthy. This became her unconscious idea of herself, and when anything went wrong in her life, that idea of herself as unworthy bubbled up and seemed real. But it wasn't. "Unworthy," "not good enough," "unlovable" are all harsh, destructive lies.

When we develop a strong idea of our Self—true or false, good or bad—we project it into the world and attract people and circumstances that help that strong idea of our Self get even stronger.

More Self-love means starting with true and powerful ideas like, *God don't make junk; you are born innately worthy; other people's actions cannot diminish your worth; your innate worth is undeniable.* Until we can stand in front of our old issues and treat our Self with loving care in their presence, those issues will recur again and again. The truth is, each time our old story shows up, it is actually winking at us, encouraging us to take a deep breath and then say, "Okay, let's try responding to these old circumstances again . . . this time with more Self-love!"

Carrie's face lit up as we explored this truth. I witnessed her grow stronger right before my eyes. She sat taller. Her tears dried up. Her breath went deeper and stayed inside her longer. Carrie's eyes focused, she looked at me, and she said, "I know I can love myself more." And I said, "Yes you can."

Then she clarified, "So I shouldn't be surprised if another married man comes into my life? It's not a statement of failure? If I hold my ground and reject the old pattern—like walking out on Francisco—instead of rejecting myself, I win?" I smiled and nodded.

Her smile became bigger. "The next time, I won't beat myself up," she said. "I won't feel like a failure. I'll be ready. I'll 'wink' at myself, and when I would normally say something unkind about myself, I'll instead say, 'I am innately worthy.' I'll breathe deep, walk away first, and reach out and give myself a good hug."

As Carrie crossed over the threshold of my office into her life, she turned back and said, "I may not be done with this just yet, but I know what I have to do to heal it." Carrie left, and I turned to remove her wadded-up tissues from the floor. For a moment, I imagined them as big fat precious pearls. How exquisite.

Inner Fitness Practice

The Big Lie

When old painful patterns occur again and again, it means you're a failure.

The Truth

Recurring events are the opportunity you need for change to occur. Harsh Self-judgment is the poison. It will live in your system until you activate the antidote of Self-acceptance and Self-love.

The Possibility

Revisiting the past as a way of forging lasting freedom from it.

Try This

1. Identify an event or pattern that keeps recurring in your life.

2. Look for the judgments and unkindness against your Self that show up in relation to that old pattern.

3. Tell your Self, *I accept and love you no matter what.* Then say something responsible and kind about your Self, like, *I am growing into my best Self; This is an opportunity for me to love my Self more; Even though I have this challenge, I deeply and profoundly love and accept my Self.*

Everything you need
is inside of you!

Do Your Circumstances Boss You Around?

When we cannot figure it out . . .
we have to give it over. It is beyond our control,
beyond our fixing, beyond our repair.
—SISTER MARY SMITH

IN THE 1990S I SPENT A NIGHT IN JAIL. THE EXPERIENCE taught me that circumstances lie.

Circumstances tell us how we are "supposed" to feel, and more often than not they give us "reasons" for feeling alone, hopeless, wronged, or all kinds of other unhappy. We think that an abusive mate, losing a job, or being confronted with illness are circumstances that make our "unhappy" legitimate, understandable. But circumstances don't have the power to dictate our lives unless we let them. My night in jail unraveled my beliefs about circumstances. Surprisingly, the circumstances did not unravel me.

I was at the tail end of an adventurous relationship with a guy whose picture you would find in the dictionary under the word *interesting*. His name was Anton. He spoke seven languages (five of them very well). He was athletic, smart, and European. He was a lot of fun.

His zest for life bulldozed his way into my then-closed life and pushed all my boundaries out, to let more light and life in. Life tends to send our way the people and lessons we need most. The challenge is to believe this and remember it, no matter how "wrong" circumstances appear to be.

Before I met Anton, big, seemingly unimportant chunks of my life were closed. Being in nature was one of them. I didn't like being outdoors. I was terrified of bugs. Outdoor adventure was something I read about but did not experience.

My relationship with Anton had me sleeping on the Nevada Salt Flats under a moon so bright that the flats glowed neon white. It took me on road trips, hiking in the Grand Canyon, skinny-dipping, bungee jumping, making love in a forest, and off-road driving. Once we even tried to cross a river in our four-wheel drive, got stuck halfway across it, and had to climb out the window of the cab before it filled with water. Yes, being with Anton was one big adventure.

Over time, however, it became clear that Anton lacked integrity in important ways. I began to see this in his dealings with other people. He used them.

He lived with me for five years, and I never saw myself as one of his artful ways to get what he wanted from others. We both benefited equally from our relationship. But the night I went to jail eliminated all benefit. That night was the dramatic awakening, death, and burial of our five years together.

It started with "circumstances" that looked like a silly 6 p.m. argument that seemed to be over a bowl of cereal. But the truth, of course, had nothing to do with cereal. We no longer fit, and our calling it quits was being drawn out.

The silly argument escalated to a drama of his knocking a carton of milk from my hand and my throwing a bowl of cereal at him. The bowl bounced off his chest and crashed to the floor. But it also clipped him under his chin and drew blood. When he saw that blood, he went berserk, hitting me a few times in my stomach with his fists. He had never been physically violent with me before. He was not a violent guy. But that night was different. I saw things I had never seen—or maybe things I had just ignored.

My mother had weathered physical violence at the hands of my father during their marriage. Watching the parts of their relationship that were unhealthy left me intolerant of a number of things, especially physical violence. I had told Anton in the beginning of our relationship that violence was my deal breaker. The punches he had just thrown broke everything between us. *(In fairness, I must say that his punches were not full punches. They did not double me over with pain or even knock the wind out of me. Anton was a black belt. His hands were lethal. Yet the back-and-forth shoulder movement I witnessed in him felt more like the anger of a little boy. I am convinced his pulled punches showed up to tell me a bigger story.)*

I told Anton he needed to pack and leave immediately or I would call the police. He challenged me by saying that if I called the police, they would take *me* to jail because he was the one bleeding. The blood revealed a nick the size and kind a man sustains while shaving. Though small, it was there nonetheless, and my angry reaction had caused it.

This was just after the O. J. Simpson trial, and law enforcement was taking domestic violence very seriously. But I did not bargain with Anton and back down. Neither did I know that he was correct about how the police would react.

* * *

As the police officers walked into the house, my German boyfriend's accent became thicker than I had ever heard it in the five years of our being together. My eyes widened listening to him as he spun a re-creation of the facts. In his story, he was a confused foreigner and bewildered by my violent, unprovoked behavior.

I listened with amazement as the police informed me that based upon the *circumstances,* they would have to "take me in" because the chin nick represented evidence of violence. I was stunned.

The officers broke protocol and kindly gave me a few minutes to prepare myself for going to jail. How does a woman who had never skipped school, never been drunk, or never even had a cup of coffee prepare for such a trip? I put on my shoes and called my mother, who I knew would call the rest of our close family. Handcuffed and sandwiched between an officer in front of me and one behind me, I left the house where I had paid the mortgage every month.

Back then, I lived in an exclusive gated community in Los Feliz. Red flashing lights shocked my neighbors as they watched me climb handcuffed into the back seat of a police car. The two officers apologized for their need to follow procedure, and we began the ride to the police station.

I was stunned by the turn of events, but oddly, I was not afraid—nor did I feel the kind of anger toward Anton that you might imagine. I found myself in these circumstances, but at the same time, I felt disconnected from them. Yes, I was in the back seat of a police car. But the years I had invested in knowing and trusting my Self meant that I was in that back seat without feeling like I was in hell.

While running the events of the previous hour through my head, my thoughts were interrupted by what would be the first of many signs that would teach me that circumstances do not dictate experience. In my years of reading spiritual books, I had come across examples of enlightened teachers knowing joy despite their difficult circumstances.

The famous psychologist Viktor Frankl came to mind. He had survived the Holocaust because he focused on his reasons for surviving as opposed to the horrific circumstances in concentration camps. I knew that how I responded to what was happening that evening would determine its effect on my life.

I had learned one thing for sure: **Hell doesn't start with our circumstances; it starts with the judgment we attack our Self with because of our circumstances.** (Examples: "I must be a fool because I made such foolish choices"; "I must be unworthy because I chose to be with someone who treats me poorly"; "I must not matter to God or in life because this thing happened to me.")

If I were to practice all I had learned, success in this situation meant I had to remember to love and accept myself as I experienced the circumstances. No feeling like a victim. No looking over the past and judging myself for being in these circumstances. No feeling like life is against me. Instead, I was prepared to see beyond these circumstances and learn their lesson.

> True lessons don't show us how we've messed up; they show us our resilience and faith.

I was pulled from the thoughts running through my mind back to the back seat of the patrol car by the whispering of one officer to the other. They were deciding where they would take me. The cop who would prove to be an angel—one of many that night—turned toward me and explained their decision to take me to a facility with far less traffic and far fewer "hardened" detainees. I thanked them and fell silent. I had learned that when it comes to challenging circumstances, the best approach is to take deep breaths to calm and center myself. And to climb into my observer's chair and watch more than react.

* * *

At the jail the two officers split up. The one who was escorting me to a holding room said, "Don't worry, I'm going to write this up in your favor." He was a wingless angel. When he deposited me in a holding area, I thanked him, and he left. Then I breathed deeply and gave thanks to that force which I could not see with my eyes but felt undeniably.

A young female officer came in, took one look at me, scrunched her eyebrows together, and declared, "You don't belong here!" Those were her words before she had asked me anything. When I told her the events as I had experienced them, she excused herself.

When she returned, she was visibly annoyed. She had called my home to give Anton the opportunity to say something that would make this all go away, but he chose not to assist in that way. The female officer was forced to send me to another facility where I would be fingerprinted, cavity searched, and booked. She was very apologetic. I thanked her for her concern and effort.

The same two cops drove me to the other facility. On this drive, thinking about the kindness I had experienced from all, I had the profound awareness that we are never alone in our circumstances. No matter what it looks like.

This evening would prove to me that there is a part in each of us that can never be hurt, harmed, or endangered. This part is our infinite SELF—eternal life itself. Even in the worst circumstances, this part of us lives. It will show up when we acknowledge it. Acknowledging this SELF can start at any moment of any day.

Acknowledgment is a way of saying to any circumstance, *I am more than this; my faith is greater than these circumstances.* When we know this, circumstances have no power to control us. They become details to be addressed or managed.

Detached from the circumstances I could feel the truth and experience its flow in my life.

When we arrived at the second jail facility, it definitely felt like jail. The intake officer was a big, intimidating woman. The intimidation was punctuated by the positioning of her intake desk and computer above me where I stood so I had to look up to her as she asked her questions.

My answer to each of her questions was no, no, no. She spoke the first three words of her final question, and I answered "NO!" before she completed it. She leveled her eyes on me and challenged me, "You don't know what I was going to ask." I said, "You were going to ask if I have ever been arrested before, and the answer is NO!" She seemed to size me up, and then in a tone that felt like it was meant to produce fear, she said, "Well then, let me ask you this . . . are you scared?"

So much happened in between the seconds of her snidely asked question and my answer. I felt a rush inside as though every part of me was gathering myself. I looked her in her eyes and spoke to her not from fear but from openness: "Should I be scared?" My question softened her, and I got a glimpse of her heart. She shook her head and said "no." I then said, with unexpected tears streaming down my face, "I am not afraid because I know who I am, and I know I am not alone."

With these words, I was overcome by both sadness and unanticipated joy. The sadness was undeniably present, yet I felt whole even in those circumstances. I knew life wasn't happening *to* me. It wasn't attacking me. Life was simply happening. It wasn't personal.

This reality was empowering: I would never again have to view any challenging event as personal. I was experiencing firsthand the opportunity we all have to practice seeing our Self empowered and whole no matter the circumstances. Every spiritual book, every church sermon, every empowerment workshop, and every word of wisdom I had reached to receive was paying dividends. And as the night would wear on, I would become even more emboldened.

They did the cavity search. When I was fingerprinted, my heart hurt. I did not want to be fingerprinted. I did not want to have a record. I did not want this brush with the "system," which can be harsh and unforgiving and long in memory and uncaring of the facts. I had to breathe deeply and accept this part. When I worried that this might cast me in a bad light to some, I heard this message from deep within: "Trust your Self."

They placed me in another holding area that had a broken phone in it. I was momentarily excited because I wanted desperately to call my family. A number of women from the night's "catch" (as the officers called it) were marched past me—talking loudly and cursing. Some were clearly intoxicated. One had a deep, rattling cough.

When my intake officer came to move me to the community wing, the sound of my voice surprised me as I impulsively said to her, "I'm sorry, but I can't go into a cell with those ladies." She looked at me like I had lost my mind. The glimpse of her heart I saw earlier was gone. The woman before me now was an underpaid county worker who had seen it all and didn't care much anymore.

Full of attitude she asked, "What do you mean you can't go in there?" I held up my finger and pointed toward the direction of a nasty cough that came on cue. "I can't afford to get sick," I said. "I earn my living with my voice. If I get sick I can't work." It was the truth. As an actress, I also work often as a voiceover artist. If I am sick, I cannot work.

You would have thought I was the strangest, most fascinating bug the way that woman looked at me and moved her head back and forth trying to make sense of what I was saying. I could literally see the inner collision of her habit with her humanity. She huffed, asked me whether I thought I was in a hotel, and then stalked away.

Ten or fifteen minutes later I was moved to the empty C Wing, which was down a hall in the opposite direction of the night's catch, the coughing and loud, incoherent voices. Before the male officer closed the cell door behind me, I noticed a large contraption thirty or forty feet away. Curious, I asked what it was. He answered, "A phone," and rolled it to me before shutting my cell door.

How had I landed here—not in jail, but in a sense of myself that could dare to believe that despite circumstances, I could ask for what I want and dare to leave my heart open to good things happening? Sitting in my own prison wing using a phone when I most wanted to call my family was evidence that I was connected to something greater than my circumstances, greater than me.

Indeed, as all spiritual teachers have said, a force greater than us exists and cares for us and responds to our heart. This force makes us innately bigger than any challenge we face. Our job is to challenge our circumstances with this kind of a response. Look at the circumstances and say, "You do not dictate my life."

* * *

This story does go on in beautiful ways. Hopefully you and I will meet at one of my Inner Fitness workshops and I will be able to share the rest of the details. Here's the thumbnail version. It seemed for a moment that I would have to come up with $50,000 for bail or $5,000 if I used a bail bondsman. I can be quite a miser when it comes to price tags that I feel are outrageous. There was no way I was going to pay $5,000 to a bail bondsman, because when this insane set of circumstances righted itself, I would still be out $5,000. I had the full $50,000 in my stock portfolio, but I couldn't get my hands on it from jail.

As I sat in my cell contemplating who to call, or what to do next, I remembered one of my favorite past spiritual revelations: If a thing is not present, it is not necessary. I had come to believe that everything we truly need is provided. Sometimes we worry that something we think we need is not there. I have learned that if that thing—in my case $50,000—is not present, then even though we think we need it, another way will be provided.

It turns out that my niece Terra had already spoken to the detective assigned to my case. After Terra had given her some details that were corroborated by the police report, that detective was incensed that I was behind bars. She told Terra to tell me not to try to bail myself out and to hang in there; she would have me out by noon—fewer than eight hours. I didn't need that $50,000 after all.

I had been developing a spiritual perspective for close to twenty years when this happened to me. I had worked and struggled to find and develop a relationship with my Self. I had worked to adopt more empowering beliefs. My efforts in these directions over the years had proved their value before that night in jail. But that night was special. It was full of angels and gifts that would sustain me forever. My night in jail is my favorite testimony to the fact that there is a force greater than us that cares for us and responds to us. That night allowed me to know beyond the shadow of a doubt that what spiritual teachers have taught is true.

* * *

We each will have our own mountaintop experience if we invest in knowing our Self. As we grow in our Self-love and Self-acceptance, our new wholeness moves us beyond the habit of harsh Self-judgment or Self-rejection.

When we know our Self, we are empowered. When we accept our Self, we are invincible . . . truly. My dramatic breakup with Anton confirmed that he came into my life to help me expand. He left me with a love of nature, and an even deeper and more profound love of my Self.

Today, I hike four to five times a week. I live on a canyon full of creepy crawly things. Deer visit my backyard at dawn. During the day, the doors of my house are usually wide open. And the door to my faith just keeps opening wider and wider.

I love my Self. I love my life.

Inner Fitness Practice

The Big Lie
Circumstances dictate reality.

The Truth
There is no circumstance bigger than the infinite
SELF that lives within you.

The Possibility
Feeling inwardly capable of meeting any circumstance
with faith, power, and resilience.

Try This
Memorize and contemplate these concepts with
curiosity:

1. I am connected to and part of a force bigger than
   me that cares for me and responds to my heart.

2. This makes me innately bigger than any challenge
   I face.

3. There is never, ever a justifiable reason to harshly judge my Self—not for any reason, under any circumstances. It is simply unacceptable.

There is a force greater than you that cares for you and responds to your heart.

Living Your Truth

Yes, you can!

A DEAR FRIEND AND I HAVE A JOKE BETWEEN US. WE SAY we wish that we could make the bed and clean the house just once, and then never have to do so again. It's a lovely thought. But living life requires cleaning; otherwise, the mess will bury us.

Life requires sorting things out, cleaning things up, moving things around—over and over. There's no overnight success when it comes to navigating life. There's no pill that transforms life's sticky mess.

If we aim to craft a fulfilling life, there's no getting around putting in a Self-centered effort. No matter how silver the spoon you may have been born with, or how loving the family you were born into, or how beautiful your body is, lies come crashing in. We all experience the hurts, dramas, traumas, upsets, disappointments, and fears that come with life. It's part of being human.

Successfully navigating this "stuff" takes work. It takes developing a thriving inner Self that can stand up to the lies. That Self lives within everyone. The job of those of us who want it is to go after this idea. Pursue it with passion. Be determined to uncover something truly beautiful from it.

In the biography *Steve Jobs*, author Walter Isaacson assigns to Steve Jobs a couple of sentences that I love. They seem to epitomize how Jobs thought about what others might have seen as impossible: "Yes, you can do it. Get your mind around it. You can do it."

This is the spirit you must embrace as you face the work of building your inner fitness and letting go of lies: "Yes, you can do it. Get your mind around it. You can do it." You can build a remarkable relationship with your Self and create a life of your dreams. Instead of the unproductive statements you have been telling yourself, I suggest that you sit with these statements for a while:

- I can disconnect from the lies I have been telling myself.
- I can wake up from the misperceptions that are burdening me.

- I can realize my value and worth.
- I can feel safe, seen, and heard in my own skin.

Deep contemplation of any one or all of these statements is a powerful way to take action and activate change in your life. Adding "How can I" to the front of each statement and asking that question, out loud with an open hopeful heart, will serve to connect you to your SELF and transform any lie and every area of your life.

- How can I disconnect from the lies I have been telling myself?
- How can I wake up from the misperceptions that are burdening me?
- How can I realize my value and worth?
- How can I feel safe, seen, and heard in my own skin?

***

"Yes, you can do it. Get your mind around it. You can do it."

This is not only possible. It is the truth!

ACKNOWLEDGMENTS

I give a very special thanks to my mother, Dorothy Lifford, and my sister Pam Lifford, who have listened to me even when they were tired; to Marty Jones, whose big sister love sustains me; and to my entire family and circle of friends who I am certain often feel as though having me in their lives is like a lifelong personal development workshop, like it or not. Your loving indulgence and generosities hone me. A heartfelt thank you goes to my dear friend, writing coach, and champion Darlene Hayes, whose words helped me turn the corner every time. Another important thank you goes to my childhood friend Frieda Richmond-Morris, whose keen ear helps me navigate and whose every word I trust. I feel the same about my friend Deborah Stewart and her listening ears and unwavering support. A big thank you goes to my other mentors and friends: Michael Beckwith, Deirdre Dix, Cynthia James, Carlyle King, Susan Cole Hill, Nick Rafter, Judy Smith, and Kevin Sullivan, whose support keeps me demanding more of myself. Special thanks goes to Shelly Balance-Ellis, Chemin Bernard, Shanna Bright, Melba Farquhar, Chuva Featherstone, Avis Frazier-Thomas, Greta Gahl, Bibi Goldstein, Tina Hiatt, Patricia Holmes, Cynthia Kemp, Celeste Moore, Mitch Newman, and Lisa Simmons, who read these stories and gave me valuable feedback. Heartfelt appreciation goes to Deborah Brown and Jackie Parker, who took the stories and, with an eye toward the essential, helped me turn them into a living, breathing self-published book in 2012. Today, my biggest thank you goes to journalist and philanthropist Shaun Robinson, who, as a stranger to me, showed up to one of my events, was touched by my self-published version of this book, and sent it to her friend, Patrik Henry Bass, at HarperCollins. Deep gratitude goes to my now editor and new friend Patrik, whose love for this book makes me smile; my sharp-eyed and loving agent, Johanna Castillo, who keeps her eye on the prize; and the entire HarperCollins team that has graciously embraced *The Little Book of Big Lies* and its possibilities. Finally, never-ending awe and love well up as I look back on the love and patience, trust and words that the Infinite SELF—God—unwaveringly extended to me. I look at this book and am humbled by what was given to me to do. I thank myself for showing up for my Self, doing the work, and trying again and again (fifty times) to write something meaningful.

Thank you for caring about your Self and joining the inner fitness movement!

#INNERFITNESS JOURNEY— SNAPSHOT

"Be fully alive!" —*Tina Lifford*

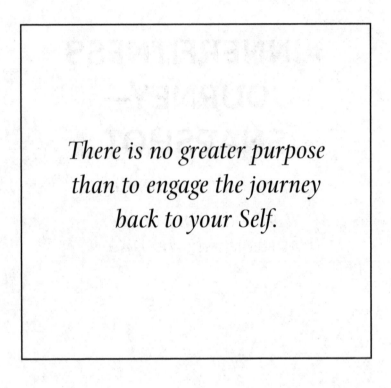

There is no greater purpose than to engage the journey back to your Self.

Go to TheInnerFitnessProject.com
or Join the Movement at IG: TinaLifford

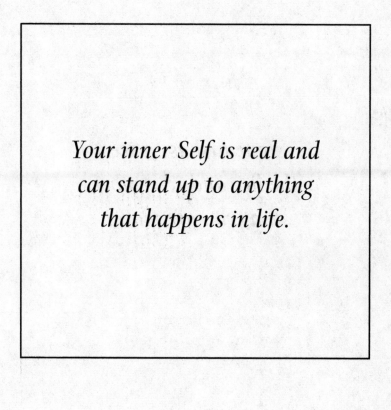

Your inner Self is real and can stand up to anything that happens in life.

Go to TheInnerFitnessProject.com
or Join the Movement at IG: TinaLifford

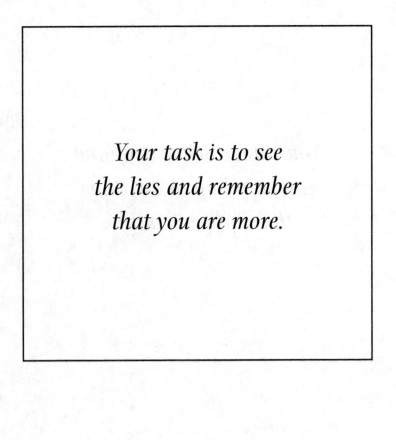

*Your task is to see
the lies and remember
that you are more.*

Go to TheInnerFitnessProject.com
or Join the Movement at IG: TinaLifford

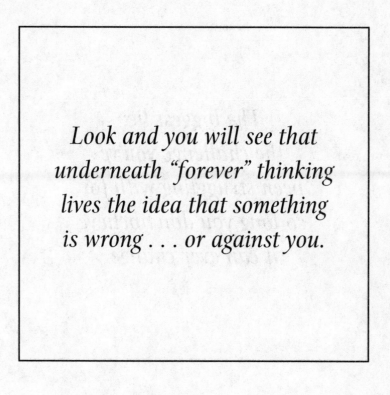

Look and you will see that underneath "forever" thinking lives the idea that something is wrong . . . or against you.

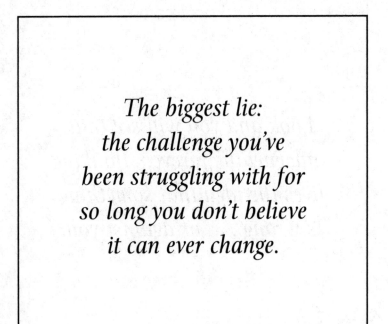

*The biggest lie:
the challenge you've
been struggling with for
so long you don't believe
it can ever change.*

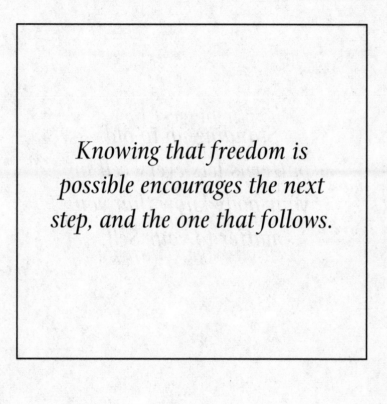

Knowing that freedom is possible encourages the next step, and the one that follows.

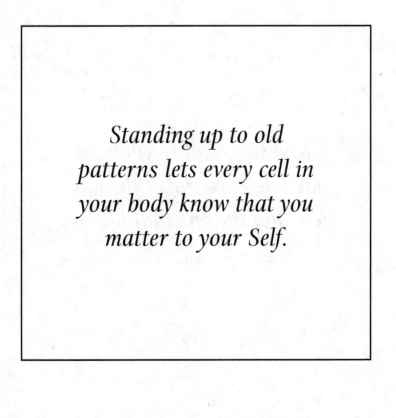

Standing up to old patterns lets every cell in your body know that you matter to your Self.

Go to TheInnerFitnessProject.com
or Join the Movement at IG: TinaLifford

When you know you matter, you can tell your Self the truth in ways that nurture Self-care.

Go to TheInnerFitnessProject.com
or Join the Movement at IG: TinaLifford

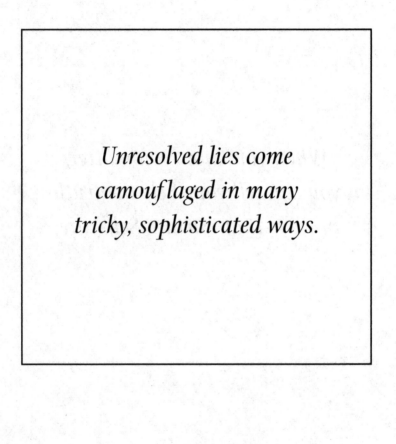

Unresolved lies come camouflaged in many tricky, sophisticated ways.

Go to TheInnerFitnessProject.com
or Join the Movement at IG: TinaLifford

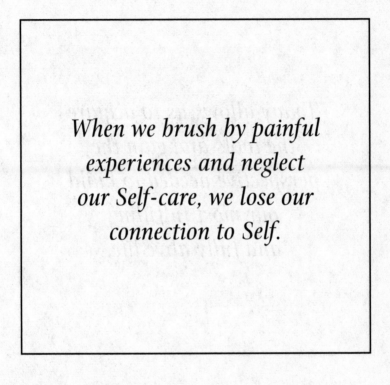

When we brush by painful experiences and neglect our Self-care, we lose our connection to Self.

Go to TheInnerFitnessProject.com
or Join the Movement at IG: TinaLifford

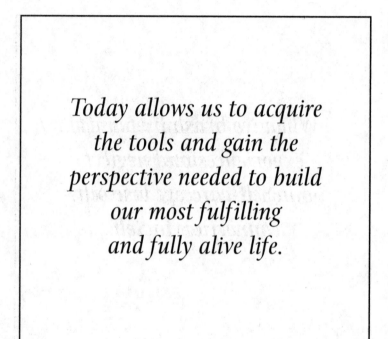

Today allows us to acquire the tools and gain the perspective needed to build our most fulfilling and fully alive life.

Go to TheInnerFitnessProject.com
or Join the Movement at IG: TinaLifford

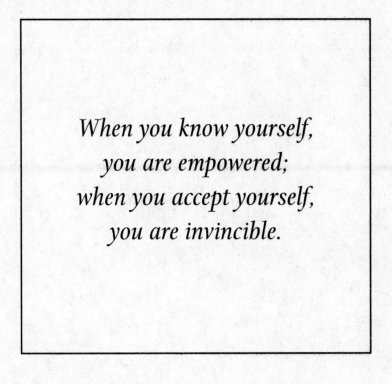

*When you know yourself,
you are empowered;
when you accept yourself,
you are invincible.*

Go to TheInnerFitnessProject.com
or Join the Movement at IG: TinaLifford

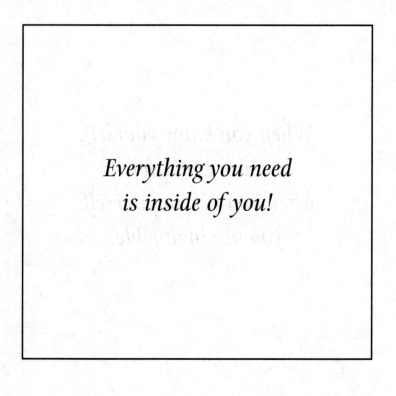

*Everything you need
is inside of you!*

Go to TheInnerFitnessProject.com
or Join the Movement at IG: TinaLifford

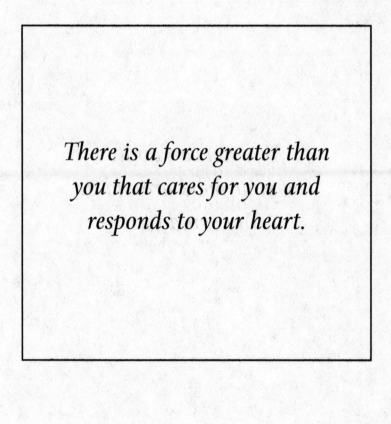

There is a force greater than you that cares for you and responds to your heart.

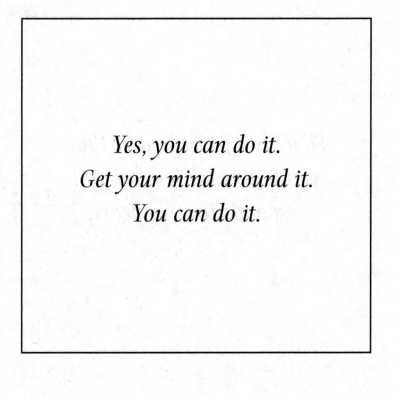

Yes, you can do it.
Get your mind around it.
You can do it.

Go to TheInnerFitnessProject.com
or Join the Movement at IG: TinaLifford

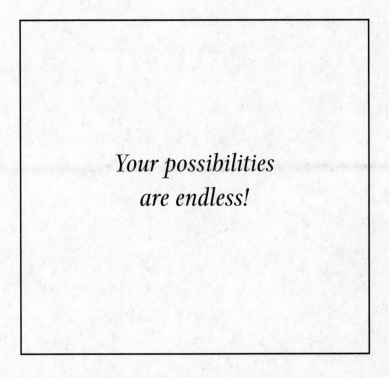

*Your possibilities
are endless!*

Go to TheInnerFitnessProject.com
or Join the Movement at IG: TinaLifford

GLOSSARY

EFT—acronym for Emotional Freedom Technique developed by Gary Craig. It is a process of tapping on different meridian points on the face and body in order to relieve stress and facilitate repairing emotional flow. (Google it for free training sessions.)

God—(synonyms) infinite SELF, SELF, Self, higher power, force, universal intelligence.

hurts, dramas, traumas, upsets, disappointments, and fears—lies that crash into our lives and make us feel small or fearful and limit our sense of what's possible for our lives.

infinite SELF (all caps)—highest SELF—God within us. It is the never-ending, uninterruptable SELF that has existed throughout time and that all things come from. SELF courses through all life and everything. It stands before life unaffected by the chaos of human confusion and fear.

inner fitness—the development and practice of inner skills that support mental, emotional, and spiritual wellbeing by expanding awareness, fostering resilience, and helping resolve unresolved issues so that we can thrive as our true Self.

lie—a false or inaccurate statement, belief, perspective, or impression that belies our innate wholeness and worth.

observer's chair—when we set an intention with our Self to objectively observe our surviving self in action and catch sight of habitual negative or unsupportive behaviors and attitudes, we imagine ourselves sitting in the observer's chair. This is a great way to become conscious of the unconscious things we believe, do, say, or think.

pain-pattern (pain-body)—chronic emotional pain that develops a life all its own inside of us. Once created, our pain-pattern (pain-body) fights to stay alive in us. The food it requires is more of the same kind of pain that created it.

sacred torture—an intimidating or painful thought or past experience that we hold on to and that seems to have a life all its own.

Self-care—acknowledging and honoring our innate worth and tending to the needs of the inner Self.

surviving self (lowercase s)—is quick to judge and take things personally and is always ready for a fight—attacking, proving, protecting, or blaming itself or others. It thinks that the image it sees in the mirror is all that it is and therefore fears for its life.

thriving Self (capital S)—sees every situation as an opportunity to grow and expand and believes that anything and everything can change for the better. It dwells in energies such as hope, possibility, enthusiasm, and gratitude.

"up until now" and *"from this point forward"*—we can use these phrases to acknowledge how things have been *up until now* yet then pivot toward what is possible *from this point forward.* This way of thinking opens a door where hope has been lost.

ABOUT THE
INNER FITNESS PROJECT™

The Inner Fitness Project is a personal development network, with the mission of gathering, designing, and teaching effective and reliable inner practices for navigating the past, present, and future with resilience, power, and vision. Using as a template the physical fitness movement that began in the 1930s, The Inner Fitness Project seeks to identify and boil down the basic components of inner fitness the way that physical fitness boils down to diet and exercise.

We believe that inner health and a profound sense of well-being are the currency of the future. People who can learn today to skillfully navigate their inner challenges will be the thriving winners in life tomorrow. Through books, workshops, a touring play, and online products, The Inner Fitness Project is making a difference in the lives of people who yearn to thrive, not simply survive.

ABOUT THE AUTHOR

Tina Lifford began her acting career in 1983. Since then, her multifaceted career has left an imprint on audiences worldwide. She currently plays Aunt Vi on OWN: The Oprah Winfrey Network's hit television show *Queen Sugar*. She is also a recognized playwright and CEO of The Inner Fitness Project, a personal development network that teaches individuals to focus more on thriving than on surviving. She desires to inspire people from all walks of life to invest in their emotional wellbeing and act on their dreams so that they can feel less stressed and respond to life with more personal power, insight, and wisdom.